Joy in Our Weakness

Joy
in our
Weakness

A Gift of Hope from the
Book of Revelation

Marva J. Dawn

SAINT LOUIS

Copyright © 1994 Concordia Publishing House
3558 S. Jefferson Avenue, St. Louis, MO 63118-3968

Library of Congress Cataloging-in-Publication Data

Dawn, Marva J.
    Joy in our weakness: a gift of hope from the book of Revelation / Marva J. Dawn.
        ISBN 0-570-04638-6
        1. Bible. N.T. Revelation—Commentaries. I. Title.
        BS2825.3.D38 1994
        228' .06—dc20   93-4500

1 2 3 4 5 6 7 8 9 10   03 02 01 00 99 98 97 96 95 94

*Dedicated to all those who suffer
from chronic and terminal illness,
from handicaps and impairments and age,
from loneliness and fears and misfortunes,
and from the misunderstandings and misstatements
of the well meaning,*

*and especially to Linden and Tim
and to our spouses, Brenda, Debbie, and Myron*

Contents

Preface   9

1. We Do Not Have to Be Afraid of The Revelation   13

2. The Gift of Weakness   21

3. God Is God, and We Are Wee   28

4. A Vision to Sustain Us in Suffering: The "Mysterious
   Purposes" of God (Rev. 1:1–3, 9–11)   35

5. Who Is Christ for Our Suffering? (Rev. 1:4–8)   43

6. Who Is the Son of Man? (Rev. 1:12–20)   49

7. Flaws and Virtues (Rev. 2–3)   57

8. Ephesus: Losing Our First Love (Rev. 2:1–7)   63

9. Smyrna: Limitations of Suffering (Rev. 2:8–11)   68

10. Pergamum: The Importance of the Word (Rev. 2:12–17)   75

11. Thyatira: True Authority (Rev. 2:18–29)   82

12. Sardis: A Call to Constant Renewal (Rev. 3:1–6)   89

13. Philadelphia: An Open Door (Rev. 3:7–13)   95

14. Laodicea: Whatever Our Limitations, We Don't Have
    to Be Tepid (Rev. 3:14–22)   101

15. The First Reason for Praise: The Gift of Life (Rev. 4:1–11)   109

16. The Second Reason for Praise: The Lamb Who Saves
    by Suffering (Rev. 5:1–14)   116

17. Don't Forget the First Horse of the Apocalypse!
    (Rev. 6:1–7:8; 19:11–21)   122

18. Endurance: The Meaning of Biblical Patience
    (Rev. 6:9–11; 7:9, 13–15)   128

19. The Third Reason for Praise: Hope for the Future
    (Rev. 7:9–17)   135

20. Skills to Read The Revelation: Silence and Trust
    in God's Vindication (Rev. 8)   141

21. The Persistence of Sin and the Immensity of Grace
    (Rev. 8:6–9:21)   148

22. Asking the Right Questions in Our Suffering:
    "How Long?" and "Meanwhile?" (Rev. 10:1–11:13)   153

23. 42 Months, 1,260 Days, and 3½ Years (Rev. 11:14–12:17)   161
24. Taking the Presence of Evil Seriously (Rev. 13–14)   168
25. We Wouldn't Want Love without Holiness (Rev. 15–16)   176
26. Fallen! Fallen Is Babylon the Great! (Rev. 17–18)   182
27. Preludes and Wedding Songs (Rev. 19:1–10)   189
28. The Ultimate Defeat of the Powers of Evil and
    the Present Reign of Christ (Rev. 20:1–21:8)   195
29. The Beautiful City: An Agent of Healing (Rev. 21:9–22:7)   204
30. "Come!": Living Now in the Coming Victory
    (Rev. 22:8–21)   211
31. Qualities for a Theology of Weakness: Perspectives
    from The Revelation on Suffering   218
Bibliography   223

The praises
of the sick
and the
broken
excuse the
silence of
the healthy
and
whole.

Rabbi Moshe Hakotun

Preface

I write this book for you, for me, and for all of us who together make up the body of Christ. The book of Revelation will enable us all to find Joy[1] in every circumstance of our lives.

I write as one who is weak and not weak enough. I struggle with physical handicaps enough to know their great benefits for the Christian life, but am not weak enough yet to accept their pain gladly. My brittle diabetes defies all the rules for taking care of its rapid blood-sugar swings. It is scary, life-threatening, immobilizing. A crippled leg, frequent foot wounds and hand surgeries, constant intestinal pain caused by nerve dysfunction and the scar tissue from an intussusception, increasing blindness, a deaf ear, and other deficiencies and deteriorations keep reminding me of a doctor's words a decade ago: "Let's face it. You have a debilitating disease; you've had it a long time. It is downhill from here . . ." How can people with chronic illness cope?

Obviously I am weak, but physical handicaps alone do not suffice to teach me how weak I truly am. At times I am deeply aware of the feebleness of my Christian life, and yet far too often I fall into the trap of thinking that somehow by my own "great effort" I can accomplish the purposes of God.

Because I am weak and not weak enough, this book is written from two sides. As one who is handicapped, I plead for all of us to learn better to care for, and listen to, each other and especially the ones who struggle with particular physical and mental challenges. On the other hand, my calls to repentance are written by one who needs this prodding.

A theology of weakness emphasizes that each of us is helpless in our sin and desperately in need of God's grace. However, because of our physical and mental capabilities, we are usually unable even to recognize—much less to acknowledge—how helpless we are. We need a theology of weakness to

9

remind us that our relationship with God is utterly dependent on his infinite grace and mercy. Only through total reliance on that grace are we able to live as God's servants in the world.

Consequently, a theology of weakness also realizes that those who accept their weakness and acknowledge their dependence can teach us best about the grace that invades all of our lives. Therefore, this theology challenges our churches to encourage the gifts and teaching potential of those who suffer and to become more truly a Christian community caring deeply about each person.

This book is also about "The Revelation of Jesus Christ" (the title in the original Greek for the last book of the Bible). This title reminds us that by grace God revealed through his servant John the truth about the lordship of Jesus to comfort people who were powerless against Roman persecution. Many people are uncomfortable with The Revelation for the very reason that it is filled with the paradox of weakness, in contrast to our world's stresses on efficiency and usefulness and power. We don't want to face the weaknesses in ourselves or cope with the weaknesses of others.

Furthermore, many people find The Revelation difficult because it cannot be analyzed scientifically. In our technological craving for facts, we can hardly understand a book that is flooded with images, memories, symbols, and mysteries. Consequently, we miss some of God's best promises and the comfort that God would give us through this wonderful book of hope. Our culture needs, more than any of the other theological virtues, the gift of hope. The Revelation is a book that overwhelms us with hope, but it is accessible to us only if we can acknowledge our weakness, and that is awfully hard for us. We don't want to shed our facades, our pretentiousness.

Finally, some people avoid the book of Revelation because they are frightened by the grotesque stories of supernatural warfare that are sometimes overaccentuated or falsely elaborated in anticipation of the end of time. While some Christians claim an infallible knowledge for pinning down the explicit meaning of each symbol in The Revelation, others ignore the last book of the Bible to stay away from the fray over its contents. The whole business is too disruptive and too mysterious.

Participants in my classes and retreats on The Revelation have urged me to write a commentary on the book, but good ones already exist. Instead, this is a book about suffering—using The Revelation for a text to invite everyone, Christian and non-Christian alike, to explore the value of its message for the 20th century. Many retreat participants have offered perspectives and criticisms, arguments and questions, to clarify my thinking as we explored this unique message together. Please do the same. Pass this book around to all your friends, discuss it over lunch at your job, struggle with its questions for your own spiritual discipline, consider its theology and application to your personal and social and religious life (whatever form the latter might take). The Revelation contains questions that apply to that dimension of everyone's existence that is manifested in our allegiance to something—anything—with an ultimate commitment.

The value of The Revelation for everybody is that it portrays the lordship of Christ. One of its great themes (often missed) is that Christ reigns especially in the midst of our suffering.

In my experience, some of the Christians who have understood best what that reign means have been disabled people or people with other limitations that force them to live out of weakness. In their suffering they have learned enormous lessons usually ignored by a culture that focuses on power and "macho" success. People who have learned to trust God in their physical challenges or other struggles, therefore, often render us all a great service by teaching us a theology of weakness sometimes lost in a triumphalistic gospel.

The Revelation invites us to learn a theology of weakness. My major hope is that all of us in the body of Christ could learn that theology better by receiving the teaching that our sufferings bring us and valuing more thoroughly the contributions that those who suffer bring to our communities. This book, thus, has a double reason for existence: it pleads with churches to discover the gifts of the weak among us, and it offers encouragement to all of us both to recognize the value of dependence in our sufferings and to offer those insights and perspectives freely to deepen the faith of our communities.

This book is dedicated to two people who have especially taught me from their weakness. Linden, a quadriplegic, and Tim, who lives by means of three weekly sessions on a kidney dialysis machine, are two of the most strongly gentle men I've ever known.

(My precious husband is a third.) I can see the reign of Christ in their lives. I owe them an enormous debt of gratitude for their input when I wrote the first draft of this book a dozen years ago, for their wise and supportive friendships, for their profound (and unromanticized) love and affection, for their gutsy courage in encountering the world.

As representatives of many other physically challenged people who have been a part of this book, I thank especially these two: Connie Kramer, who gave me out of her visual impairment a story of grace when I was depressed about possible amputation of my foot; and Karyl Groeneveld, who, in spite of severe pain from chronic back problems, does wonderful research for me. For example, she provided information on *tephillin* for chapter 24 of this book.

I also give great thanks to my former secretary, Sandy Drees, who first gave me space and time in her home and heart to get excited about the possibilities of this book and to begin fleshing out its contents; to Leonard and Odessa Johnson, who gave me refuge (literally, since a tornado came frighteningly close) to finish the rough draft; and to Holy Trinity Lutheran Church, Elmira, New York, who hosted a teaching conference on The Revelation and who provided financial aid to give me a month off from teaching to begin working on revisions.

Marva J. Dawn
The Day before Easter

Note

1. In all my writing I capitalize the word *Joy* in order to invite readers to pause and be reminded that our relationship with God fills us with security, confidence, and hope. Joy is the deep sense of God's sustaining presence, the realization that his light is greater than any darkness that might temporarily assail us. Thus, Joy does not mean "happiness," which is dependent on human circumstances. This distinction is elucidated more thoroughly in chapter 12 of my book on Psalms, *I'm Lonely, Lord—How Long?* (Harper and Row, 1983).

1

We Do Not Have to Be Afraid of The Revelation

The lecturer had everything pinned down. On that day 10 years ago, he knew exactly what events of world history were prophesied by which images in the book of Revelation so that he could plot on a timeline exactly how close we were to the end of the world. His perspective fit in well with the contemporary situation of nuclear madness and economic chaos, so his listeners were both terrorized and strangely comforted by his predictions. Though the tribulation would be ghastly (Armageddon in terms of megatonned radioactivity), at least Communist evil would finally be punished and American justice would prevail. Meanwhile, he insisted, the job of Christians is to tell others that noticeable events, such as the eruption of Mount St. Helens and the severe droughts of previous summers, are signs of the imminent end, to which the world ought to pay attention in order to repent.

A careful study of The Revelation will demonstrate that this is not the primary message of the book. Rather, its symbols and images affirm the truth that victory lies in weakness. Such an interpretation invites us to turn to the last book of the Bible when things are hard—when we are struggling with illness or harassment at work, with financial shortages or other family difficulties. Such a perspective really offers profound comfort and hope.

The Revelation itself invites our careful study. It is the only biblical book that both begins and ends with a promise to those who pay attention to its message. At the beginning, the seer St. John testifies that everything he saw is truly the Word of God and the testimony of Jesus Christ, and then he proclaims, "Blessed is the one reading and those hearing the words of the prophecy and heeding the things which are written in it, for the time is near" (Rev. 1:3). Similarly, at the book's end, the one who is coming soon gives this promise: "Blessed is the one heeding the words of the prophecy of this book" (22:7). Certainly these promises invite us to search for insight into this precious, mysterious book. Its visions will give us a new understanding of life and suffering and the significance of our religious yearnings.

In an interesting experiment conducted before the era of *glasnost*, U.S. school children were shown pictures of tree-lined streets and asked why the Russians planted trees like that. The children responded, "So people won't be able to see what's going on beyond the road" or "to make work for prisoners." When asked why American roads have trees beside them, the same children said, "for shade" or "to keep the dust down." Everything depends on perspective.

Most important for a careful study of The Revelation is the basic perspective with which we view the book. At the outset, these four guidelines will allow our approach to preserve its artistic and theological integrity:

1. A historical perspective. The first rule for understanding any piece of literature is that we must know in what time period it was written to clarify what it meant originally for those who first read it. The most obvious danger of many interpretations of the Bible is that they begin with the 20th century and move backwards. Starting with particular events of our times, they claim to find "prophecies" that predicted them.

Of course, statements in the Scriptures are often fulfilled in times after they were written. Indeed, much of the Christian understanding of who Jesus was and what he did comes from recognizing the significance in his life of certain passages from the First Testament.[1] However, these are the second level of meaning for those Hebrew passages. Honest interpretation of the Christian Scriptures must begin with the Hebrew perspectives of the ones who wrote and of their Jewish readers. Anyone reading the previous illustration, for example, would have to keep in mind the pre-*glasnost* hostilities between the U.S.S.R. and the U.S. to interpret it appropriately.

Therefore, to be faithful to the text, we must begin by understanding the historical situation in which the book was written. Even though scholars disagree about many particulars of its external situation (such as whether the John who wrote the book was the disciple of Jesus and whether the author actually saw the visions or dreamed them), all scholars agree that the book was written during a time of persecution against the early Christians—perhaps the persecution of Nero, around 64 A.D., or of Domitian, between 81 and 96 A.D.

To begin with the first century as opposed to the 20th makes a huge difference in the ordering of our theological work and, therefore, in its accuracy. First, from the book we gather data, what the text said to the people at the time of its writing, and then we can more faithfully deduce what implications that message might have for us. Such an approach deals more truly with the text than an approach that begins with our situation and then forces 20th-century perspectives onto first-century minds. To study the Scriptures with historical integrity means to judge them in their own time and place and to take literally their original message for the original readers.

Our approach in this book, then, will be to understand a passage as did the earliest Christians, to formulate from their situation the principles conveyed by the text, and only then to apply those principles to our times.

2. Literary purposes. This aspect naturally follows from the preceding. If we are looking at The Revelation for what it said in a historical situation of persecution, we will search for why it was written and the way in which it was written.

In one conference on The Revelation, I asked the participants to gather with other members of their families to talk about some situation of great fear in which its resolution taught them an important lesson about the love of God. Then they were to prepare a sentence to intrigue the rest of us and to remind their own family of the meaning of the event.

One family delighted us all with this summary: "Don't worry! The police will bring him back." Everyone in the room couldn't wait to hear the story.

One day their toddler had wandered away from home during rush hour, had safely crossed one of the busiest highways in their city, and was found about two miles from home by a policeman who could return him because of the brand-new identification bracelet on his wrist. Can you imagine that family's relief when the policeman brought him unharmed to their door and told them where he had been found? The coded message, "Don't worry! The police will bring him back," reminded that family of an instance of God's immense care—and now, several years later, still fills me with wonder and hope and comfort.

The same literary purposes are operating in the book of Revelation. The writer addressed Christians confronting an agonizing situation. They were being persecuted—tortured, thrown to lions, burned—because they clung to the lordship of Christ. How could they have the courage to go on in the face of such suffering? How could they find hope in the midst of such terror?

The writer of The Revelation responds carefully. He, too, is a prisoner for his faith. According to his testimony, he was imprisoned on the island of Patmos, where political captives worked in the mines. The Roman government was wise (humanly speaking) to put the important leader John there. To make John a martyr would only have increased the influence of his witness. So he was sent away into slavery. His letters were most certainly censored.

How, then, could he communicate with the Christians back in Asia Minor? How could he offer them hope and comfort without his letters being destroyed by the officials who guarded him?

He wrote stories. They were crazy and bizarre stories—probably passed on as the work of a lunatic. However, they overflowed with images identifiable to the family, to those who knew the family history, for The Revelation is filled with stories and images from the First Testament and from the oral traditions of Jesus' teachings maintained in the early Christian community. Its pictures come from the traditions of Israel; they symbolize the ways in which God took care of the weak and despised Hebrews and made them his people.

The original readers of The Revelation would immediately recognize those images as well as the larger biblical passages from which they came. They would have known, for example, that the writer meant not only a lamb that was slain, but that he referred to the entire context of that image in the Passover sequence of Exodus 12. The Israelites observed that festival (as well as the Day of Atonement, which significantly used instead a lamb that was not slain) to remember God's promises of protection and reconciliation and hope for a covenant land. Just as our retreat participants' phrase suggested a lovely story of divine protection and human care, so these images from the First Testament and from oral traditions about Jesus implied the sovereignty of God and the community of his people.

This is the framework in which we must look for the central thrusts of the message in The Revelation. From these purposes we can draw applications for our times.

3. The study of literature. We all read various kinds of literature in daily life with skills appropriate to their respective literary genres. For example, we don't read comic strips with the same seriousness as editorials or as the directions of a cookbook. Similarly, when we read the Bible we use different skills to study poetry, prophecy, apocalyptic literature (defined in chapter 4), narrative, sermons, history, or liturgy. Whereas some books are easy to understand because they might contain only one type of literary form, The Revelation contains all seven. Although we will comment on various aspects of these literary styles throughout the course of this book, at this point we must address particularly the problem of prophecy. That word has distorted connotations in our times because of such foretellers as Jeanne Dixon, who predicted that President Kennedy would be assassinated. Those who believe her forecasts forget that she also missed on some major issues, such as whether or not he would be elected, if Pope Paul would enjoy good health (he died), and if the roof of the gymnasium at the University of Georgia would collapse (my brother registered there safely). Prophecy is usually defined in our modern world as foretelling the future by paranormal abilities. In contrast, we understand biblical prophecy less as a prediction of the future than as an inspired recognition of where the present course was leading.

This ties in with our second principle about literary purposes, for the writer of The Revelation was not at all foretelling distant events to comfort his friends in their present suffering. Moreover, as our first historical principle stresses, his words must certainly be applied first to that very situation of persecution and then, secondarily, to our times. St. John was clarifying for his original readers where the present course of events was leading and how they should respond to the crisis. Thus, our third point is that, literarily, prophecy in The Revelation is a critical reflection on the meaning of first-century events in light of the eternal purposes of God.

This is not to say, let me hastily add, that The Revelation might not also give us some perspective on events of our time. However, our perception of this must come after, and not before, the recognition of the original and primary purpose of biblical prophecy. When we have done a thorough job of ferreting out the meaning for a persecuted people under the Roman state, then we can draw some conclusions about applications to our times.

4. The fundamental point of view. It is necessary to remove ourselves from ordinary 20th-century ways of thinking in order to recognize the vast difference between contemporary anthropocentrism and the theocentrism of the first century. Our times are characterized by patterns of mind that begin with ourselves as the focus. These anthropocentric perspectives make humankind (the Greek word is *anthropos*) their center.

The Scriptures do not arise from such a perspective. They are written by people who began their thinking with the voice of God (*theos* is the Greek word for divinity). Notice how often throughout the Bible the writers include such notations as "thus says the LORD" or "declares the LORD." Notice also how often God is the one speaking and constantly repeating "I . . . I . . . I . . ." with various verbs of action. Anyone who reads the Scriptures carefully cannot miss this constant refrain of God speaking, God creating, God directing, God transforming, God intervening, God declaring his purposes, God loving. Everywhere the perspective is God's, so it is with his viewpoint that we must read the literature. This makes an enormous difference in the way we read The Revelation. When we view it theocentrically, we read it to learn what it says about God, not about us, and about his timing and purposes rather than ours.

Yet it is not necessary to believe in God to read it this way, just as we don't have to become like the idiot to accept his perspective in *One Flew over the Cuckoo's Nest.* However, by the end of that book we find ourselves accepting him for who he is and the transformation that has been wrought. I think that The Revelation (properly explained) is a good book for unbelievers to read in order to discover the character of God, who is the Lord of everything.

I emphasize this point because far too often Christians do not realize how subtly we are dissuaded from the theocentric perspective that should characterize faith. We live in an age of subjectivism, in which how we are experiencing things determines their reality. Subjectivism is evident in such slogans as "If it feels good, do it." Not so evident is the way subjectivism distorts our society's approach to religious phenomena. Modern interpretations of scriptural accounts center on the perceptions of the disciples rather than on what Jesus was teaching about his kingdom or on the experience of the children of Israel rather than on what Yahweh was showing them about himself. Because the 20th-century mind is characteristically inward-turned, this subjectivism has invaded our theology, as can be seen in much of contemporary Christian ethics, as well as in Christian music. A large, dramatic Easter pageant shocked me when the words from Handel's *Messiah*, "and the glory of the Lord shall be revealed," were changed to "when we shall see his glory." That shift might not seem so drastic, but think of the dichotomous difference of perspective it indicates. Now the emphasis is on how we, subjectively, are seeing God's glory, rather than on the objective fact of God's revelation.

In order to analyze properly a piece of literature, we simply must study it from the point of view from which it was written, and the Scriptures declare themselves to be God's revelation of himself. The Revelation (notice that the word is singular) literally begins as follows in the original Greek:

> *The revelation[2] of Jesus Christ, which God gave to him, to make manifest to his bond-servants the things which must necessarily take place shortly; and he communicated [these things] having sent [them] through his angel to his bond-servant John, who bore witness to the word of God and to the testimony of Jesus Christ, even to all that he saw.*

In one sentence the theocentric perspective (which includes the testimony of Jesus, clearly recognized in the book as divine) is mentioned four times.

This last element of perspective is one of the main reasons I feel compelled to write this book, for it seems to me that much of the flabbiness of contemporary Christianity derives precisely from this failure to approach things from God's perspective and to recognize the objectivity of his revelation. Later we will consider the validity of that revelation and the meaningfulness of such a perspective in a world where everyone wants to begin with him- or herself. For now let us simply agree to look at The Revelation from the perspective of its author, who states unequivocally that he has written not his own thoughts and ideas, but the very words of God and the testimony of Jesus. This leads us to some incredible results, to be noted in the next chapter.

Notes

1. I prefer to call the first three-fourths of the Bible the "First Testament" or the "Hebrew Scriptures" to avoid our culture's negative connotations of the name *Old* Testament and to emphasize the continuity of God's covenants in the Bible with Israel and Christians and the consistency of God's grace for his people.
2. The Greek word *apocalypse,* translated "revelation," will be defined more thoroughly in chapter 4.

2

The Gift of Weakness

Now that we have clarified the basic foundational perspective with which we enter into the book of Revelation, we can focus in this chapter on overviewing the main three-part theological message that the book conveys. In the next introductory chapter we will look more closely at our participation in that truth by acknowledging and valuing our weakness.

God's message to us in the book of Revelation is that in the present we are not always going to win; our lives will not always be characterized by triumph. That is a lesson hard to accept—in fact, impossible—except that it is balanced on the opposite side with this hope: eventually we will win. These poles stand in a dialectical tension and cannot be brought together because of the intervening reality of satanic opposition.

These three parts—the ultimate, cosmic lordship of God in Christ; the present opposition of the powers of evil; and the resultant suffering on the part of God's people—lead to this other important aspect of the theology of The Revelation: that meanwhile we endure with patience our weakness. The hope of God's ultimate reign sustains our longsuffering.

Many 20th-century Christians find that almost impossible to accept. Instead they have espoused a theology of "victory, healing, luxury, and blessedness" that The Revelation does *not* teach. God does not promise us a rose garden—at least not one without thorns. And though there are, of course, many roses in life, they fade, too—with the promise that they will come again next season. Life has its rhythms and fragrances.

We have to get our facts straight. We cannot ignore that we live in a world dominated by sin and not by the purposes of God. All the talk about the progress of the human race is really an illusion, as we discover when we correctly read the Scriptures and human history. We see over and over again that power corrupts, leaders

deceive, persons hurt each other for their own gains, dreams die—
or, perhaps more precisely, are usually killed. This is not just
gloomy pessimism. In fact, Christian realism is much more opti-
mistic than shallow illusions about humankind's goodness because
this genuine realism recognizes that God is working still in spite of
evidence to the contrary. His purposes will prevail in the world in
spite of all the gunk and muck.

However, the gunk and muck are there, and we do great dis-
service to those who suffer if we gloss over it and dump on them a
mindlessly "hopeful" gospel of pablum victory over their pain. The
Revelation teaches that God always gives victory eventually, but
the meanwhile entails suffering.

This message is crystal clear (see, for example, 2:10–11) in The
Revelation. It is a message we could more easily embrace if we paid
better attention to those in our midst who understand the grace of
weakness.

Let's start with the fact of evil. In his letter to the Ephesians, Paul
declares that we are battling "against the rulers, against the powers, against the world forces of this darkness, against the spiritual
forces of wickedness in the heavenly *places*" (Eph. 6:12). The book
of Revelation describes these forces in terms of dragons, beasts,
prostitutes, and the warriors of Armageddon. No matter what names
we call the powers of evil, if we do not acknowledge their reality
in the world, we foolishly deceive ourselves.

The stories in Genesis 3–11 make this point clear: human
beings, fallen from their created purposes, are no longer capable
of fulfilling God's intentions for them. Moreover, human rebellious-
ness has let loose all sorts of other evils in the world. Though that
fall has been counteracted by the work of Christ, the restoration
has not yet been completed. The letter to the Colossians declares
that in our suffering we are completing the work of Christ. Of
course, we do not participate in the work of redemption itself,
which has been thoroughly finished at the cross and empty tomb.
Rather, we "fill up what is lacking" in the work of creating the community of God's people (Col. 1:24). Even as Colossians equates
involvement in that work with the processes of our suffering, so The
Revelation comforts those who undergo suffering and even martyr-

dom in order that the work of the kingdom of God might be continued in spite of, and in opposition to, the evil that assails it.

Furthermore, the evil that dominates the world seems at times to be out of God's control. We certainly cannot know why God allows the results of sin to be manifest in such things as terminal illness or the destructive forces of nature (like the tornado that totally demolished a town 25 miles from where I originally worked on this book). Moreover, we ought to be a little bit afraid of anyone who gives too simplistic an explanation for these phenomena. Nor should we trust those who say that God must not be powerful enough to stop such evil, that he is still in the process of becoming almighty. That contradicts the constant refrain of the Scriptures that Yahweh *is* the LORD of hosts, that he *reigns* now as King of kings and Lord of lords, that his purposes eventually *will prevail* and *are prevailing* now.

Of course, these assertions do not advocate a blind faith that merely says, "Well, it doesn't look true, but we just have to believe it." We certainly do not need to sacrifice our intelligence to believe in a God who is both all-loving and all-powerful. We do, however, have to acknowledge that, since our intelligence is vastly inferior to God's, we simply cannot yet know all there is to know.

All the arguments declaring that God could not be both all-good and all-powerful and still allow such evil in the world are anthropocentric arguments.[1] If we begin instead with God and acknowledge his infinite love and power and wisdom, then we must admit that we are not able yet to figure everything out. Our response to the problem of theodicy (God's justice in the face of evil) must be that God is God and we are wee.

Beware of any answer that claims to be a total answer. Usually such approaches wind up trying to be God.

Though we cannot escape the horrendous amount of evil in the world, the good news of the Gospel is that God will not let us be defeated at the hands of sin and evil and death. Part of the meaning of the resurrection of Jesus is that God has triumphed through Christ's suffering and is continuing to go about the business of restoring this world to its original design and purposes. Though we might have to undergo intense suffering in our present times of trouble, yet after the death comes the resurrection. As Paul so wonderfully proclaims in 1 Corinthians 15, since Christ is raised, we know that we too shall rise. Death and grave, sin and evil have all lost their sting.

Yet we remain in a meanwhile time beset with the problems of sin and the results of evil. We must face those ills realistically, truthfully.

Many people try to convince those of us who are handicapped that prayer will undoubtedly restore those parts of the body that are debilitated by accident or chronic disease. I know personally—and theologically—that we are better helped by a more realistic approach. For example, Rev. Bill Vaswig conducted a healing ministry for many years under the "Life Institute for Prayer," which aroused my deep respect because he was so very compassionate. He both acknowledged the reality of evil in the world and was able to free many people from various physical ailments in his wholistic approach to healing. In his conversations on the physical benefits of prayer, he listed several kinds of illness for which he had prayed and the positive results he had seen. However, he readily admitted that in some particular problems he had never seen improvement. This experienced person of prayer with a profound ministry of confirmed healing acknowledged that healing doesn't always occur.

I do not doubt God's power. God can grant complete healing if that is his perfect purpose. However, sometimes other, more important aspects of his work are involved than just our release from physical limitations. Perhaps God can use us much more effectively in our limitations than if we were dependent on our own powers. It would be too easy to take the credit for that which is, of course, always God's work, if life were simple for us.

Why is my friend Linden still in a wheelchair? Why is Tim still on dialysis? The answer is not that God is not capable of restoring these gifted men to perfect health, but that he is using them more thoroughly in their physical limitations. Neither of them would object at this point to his purposes, even though at times they struggle with frustrations and doubts.

None of us has given up on healing. We still pray for each other's total recovery. More important, we pray for each other's "meanwhiles"—how we are coping with the situations we are in and how we can enjoy them to the hilt, in spite of the obstructions.

(Most interestingly, since I wrote the rough draft of this book, all three of us have married wonderful people.)

During my four years in graduate school in Indiana, my prayers for physically challenged friends often arose while I rode the bus to the university. My visual handicaps necessitated this mode of transportation, but the daily bus trips were made easier by the frequent presence of a cheerful blind girl, who brought bright smiles and jokes wherever she went. What a lovely model she provided of a person who has seized the meanwhile. This lesson we all need to learn from the weak in our midst (see the following chapter).

The value of our weakness is that it teaches us to wait for God's timing, to overcome evil with love, to respond with gentleness instead of violence. In our world people often try to overcome limitations with power, but power always causes resistance. We can't force someone to believe in Christ, to love us, or to think as we do. Sometimes I hear people pray as if they were twisting God's arm to force him to live up to his promises to heal. Certainly we can't accomplish God's purposes through power or trying to force his hand.

One morning I awoke with stabbing pain in my eye. It felt like something was poking it, but several persons looked and could find nothing. All efforts to force whatever was causing the irritation to come out led to greater pain and more watering. I spent the entire day trying to avoid those movements that intensified the poke, and my eye chose to water all day long—while I gave the morning Bible study at camp, ate meals, and traveled by car from Iowa to Wisconsin. Finally somehow, somewhere, at some time, the irritator was finally dislodged. All the tears had gently done their work.

We can see the same process in model human relationships. Someone acts as an enemy, but the one opposed continues to be caring and gentle. In spite of badgering, mockery, hostility, even brutality, the gentle love of God through that individual persists, until finally grace prevails and the relationship is restored. Suffering love overcomes more effectively than power.

Yet too many Christians persist in using power. We try to control governmental policies. We try to barrage with brilliance and wealth. We try to force Christianity on others and make them buy our values.

The Revelation will teach us another way. It will help us discover and understand the victory of weakness, a discipline of willingness to suffer. In our post-Christian age we are very much like the believers for whom John wrote The Revelation. Christianity is not really in charge in our culture anymore, so it must be lived in the modern world from a minority position. We are all part of a society that forgets original sin, heaven and hell, the cross, and the absolute sovereignty of God. Consequently, we cannot simply assert what we believe and compel the rest of the world to believe it, too. However, the Christian community can gently continue to live as the people of God and offer a viable alternative to the rat-race, smash-your-neighbor, violent society that surrounds us. We can live out the Gospel in peaceful, caring ways that manifest the alternative lifestyle of those who follow Jesus Christ.[2]

That model excites me because it genuinely follows the Jesus who brought healing to those who suffered and who demonstrated what it meant that the kingdom of God had come near. Then he sent out his disciples to bring the same healing and message about the kingdom to the world in which they moved. Now The Revelation asserts in several places (such as 1:6 and 5:10) that he has made us a kingdom and priests, that our work in the world is to continue to model his alien values in a power-grabbing society.

Such a perspective acknowledges, too, that there is sin in our midst. We are not always going to be successful at modeling the alternative life in Christ. At those times we model other, core dimensions of our faith—the gift that we are forgiven, the care of the Christian community to restore those who have erred, and the opportunity to work together as a people to learn anew what it means to follow Jesus. Thus, we model in our failures what to do with sinful weakness—forgive it, treat the sufferer with compassion, and work for restoration, reconciliation, and wholeness.

The healing strength of such an approach was impressed on me at a time when things seemed disastrous in my life. Newly arrived at Notre Dame, I felt overwhelmed by the brilliance of my colleagues in the Ph.D. program; the books I needed to prepare for the Greek exam were lost by the moving company; mice invaded my apartment; an injury to my foot made me hobble for three weeks; too much stress affected my eyes so that I could not read for eight days;

I lost my identification paper; my thermos bottle fell off the desk and broke; poor people were sleeping in cars in the parking lot beneath my bedroom window, and I grieved for their situation in life and felt helpless to aid them; I missed desperately all my friends on the West Coast from which I had moved; and I had a week to proofread the galleys for my book on the Psalms. I was overwhelmed by it all and did not have any close friends yet to whom I could turn.

One gentle act helped me find hope and strength to go on in my weakness. One person who noticed that I was close to tears pulled out a clean, white handkerchief and invited me to talk about whatever was troubling me. That touch of gentle kindness freed me to cry and then to go on with the struggle.

Similarly, in the turmoil and doubts brought on by our limitations and illnesses and sufferings, it is not necessarily a hyped-up promise of healing that will enable us to overcome. Usually the one who gently stands beside us, who touches us with caring, empowers us most and frees us to grow. I become more depressed when people who pray for healing harangue me about my lack of faith, which prevents it, but I find new, wholistic healing when a friend asks for God's embrace in my life.

We will best overcome hostility against us by loving. Jesus overcame the hostility of the Roman empire, the Jewish religious leaders, and the aggravated crowds by submitting to their execution and forgiving their ignorance.

If we really want to follow him, we must learn his methods for overcoming evil. And the persons from whom we can best learn those lessons are those who begin from a position of weakness.

Note

1. An excellent book that responds to all the arguments is Peter Kreeft's *Making Sense Out of Suffering* (Ann Arbor, MI: Servant Books, 1986).
2. See Marva J. Dawn, *The Hilarity of Community: Romans 12 and the Meaning of the Church* (Grand Rapids, MI: Wm. B. Eerdmans Publishing Co., 1992).

3

God Is God, and We Are Wee

Grandma's eyes always twinkled in amusement over my failure to get German pronunciation and phrasing right. Yet she patiently put up with my slowness and helped me practice the language. Her confident repetition of favorite hymns and prayers, especially in the hours before her death, inspired me when we were together and comfort me now as I remember the strength of her hope.

Grandpa Bayer, now 101, continued for years to build birdhouses and recipe holders. He rescued all sorts of junk from garbage cans and converted it into useful items. He used to gather stale bread from various grocery stores in order to feed hundreds of ducks in the wintertime. Any eggs left without mothers because of teenage vandalism of the nests were always brought immediately to his basement for hatching under a light bulb and Grandpa's gentle care until the ducklings could make it on their own in the river.

These beloved grandparents and many others like them demonstrate the countless contributions of senior citizens to the well-being of our society. Yet many "senile" patients in convalescent centers have been discarded by their families as worthless.

Studies have shown that senility (as distinguished from Alzheimer's disease) is aggravated by abuse—that those who are treated as old people are much more likely to develop the illnesses of age. They have been forgotten, and their deadened spirits are reflected in their bodies' inability to cope.

We stand aghast at the abandonment of people in our society, and yet, to some extent, all of us are guilty. We have relegated the weak and infirm and mentally deficient and aged to places of insignificance.

Today as arguments about abortion, euthanasia, racism, sexism, and ageism swirl around us, we who claim to be God's people must do some major rethinking about the place of the weak and helpless in our society and our churches. How much of a part do the handicapped, the retarded, the aged, the infants play in our Christian communities? How much do we welcome children into the world?[1] How much do we value the contributions of the old instead of wishing they wouldn't be so traditional? To our great loss, in such antagonism we lose track of the moral truths they are trying desperately to preserve—the loss of which has led to great corruptions in our society.

The Bible is always on the side of the oppressed. The prophets in the First Testament rage against those who sell the needy for a pair of sandals (Amos 8:6), those who add house to house and join field to field (Is. 5:8), thereby robbing the poor. Throughout the Scriptures God's people are warned that their harmful actions toward the weak and helpless will be paralleled by God's wrath against them. Unless they repent of their lack of care, they will lose the kingdom of God. We must recognize this inextricable connection: the kingdom of God is made up of the poor, the humble, the weak, those who suffer.

This is made especially clear in the 12th chapter of Luke. There it is recorded that Jesus said, "Sell your possessions and give mercifully," right after he said, "Do not fear, little flock, for your Father took delight to give you the kingdom" (vv. 33 and 32). In sharing the life of the poor we most richly experience the kingdom of God.

The fact that God is on the side of the oppressed is an important truth being emphasized by contemporary liberation theologians from the third world and by feminist and black theologians in the first world.[2] However, this truth about God's care for the weak and helpless is frequently distorted in theologies that do not remain biblical and that often advocate resorting to violence to accomplish their purposes. The peaceable kingdom of God can never be brought in by violence. If we want others to know its meaning, we must introduce them to its ruler: the Lamb that was slain. If we want to follow Jesus, then we must take up our cross, which does not mean to suffer some minor inconvenience, but to shoulder the crosspiece on which we will die.

We can learn best about the redemptive power of suffering from those who can accept it even if it is imposed on them without their choice. One of my goals in this book is to encourage us all to value the gifts of the infirm instead of trying to change them. How can we as the body of Christ learn better to welcome them into the community and encourage them to offer their gifts?

Tim and Linden and I have often laughed at how many times people say to us that our physical situations could be changed if we would just learn to pray "right" or if we had stronger faith. I spent years trying to "grow" my faith so that it could convince God to grant me healing in response to my frequent petitions. I do believe in miraculous healing, for I experienced it several years ago when my intestine had intussuscepted and strangled itself. The nurses couldn't believe how rapidly my body recuperated, but I knew it was in response to the prayers of many friends around the country. Other physical situations have revealed to me the power available in God's timing and in the caring support of God's people along the way. However, God's best plan has not been to grant me total release from my health problems, even as his plan for Paul included the retention of the thorn in the flesh.

The problem has been much worse for friends whose physical limitations are more obvious. Countless times Linden has been approached by people who insist that he could get out of his wheelchair if he would just submit to their prayers (as if these people had some sort of magic touch). How obnoxious!

Though he has not given up on the possibility of a miracle, Linden told me several years ago that he greatly longed for his pastor to stop praying in public worship for his healing. Such a practice enforced the attitude in the whole congregation that he was not acceptable in their midst until he was changed. He seemed to represent a failure on their part to claim God's power sufficiently, and so they could not tolerate this weakness that reminded them of their own. How much more helpful it would have been for him—and for them—if instead they could have learned how to pray for his life in the chair meanwhile, as he waits for the final victory over sin and pain that is indeed coming. If they could have prayed for his strength and ability to cope, then they would have learned how to be a community of support for this time. Meanwhile, also, they could have begun to learn more readily from Linden all that he has to teach about the power of God in our suffering and the victory that can only come through weakness and limitations. They might have learned from him what it means totally to depend on God and to learn the sufficiency of his grace. (See chapter 18 for a more thorough explication of the biblical concept of God's grace and human patience.)

The nature of our times also makes it critically important to learn from the aged. As the values of our culture shift so much and so fast, our youth grope for something steady to hang on to. At a retreat a few years ago for senior citizens, we focused on the book of Malachi and the many principles it contains that have been lost in some contemporary churches—God's absolute prohibition against divorce, the desirability of the tithe, the importance of leaders faithful to God's Word and not seeking positions for personal gain. As I looked at the faces of the 60 senior citizens before me—all of them devoutly committed to the Lord—I was overwhelmed by the potential for clear instruction of youth if our churches would tap the wisdom of these folk.

Youth certainly are begging for such instruction. I am constantly surprised at how many youth thank me for offering them a better alternative when I speak about sexual relationships and advocate both the old-fashioned policy of sexual intercourse only within the covenanted security of lifelong marriage and also responsible tenderness in our affectionate relationships before marriage. Many teenagers in personal discussion say that they wish their parents or pastors had talked with them about the values of these biblical principles.

Every time I see announcements of anniversary parties for couples who are celebrating 50 years together, I weep with great Joy and great sadness. What a treasure to see in them the model of devoted steadfastness, of suffering love that has put up with all their struggles for all these years. I rejoice that their relationships are indeed golden. And I weep for youth today and even for my generation, for very few people in our present society are willing to put up with the suffering enough to refine their relationships into gold.

So what do all these comments mean for the people of God? Most important, we must get back to scriptural principles, to recognize as did the believers for whom the book of Revelation was written that we live in an alien world with alien values and that we are involved in spiritual warfare against beasts and dragons and the spiritual hosts of wickedness in the heavenly places. Second, we can pay more attention to those who might be able to teach us about steadfastness and commitment and longsuffering and strength in weakness, those who have battled limitations and survived.

I will never forget the first day I visited with Linden at his office in the alcohol treatment center where he was a counselor. He met me in the lobby, and, as we traveled down the hall to his office, I was impressed that he chooses not to have a motorized chair in order to force himself to exercise as he pushes his way from place to place. When we reached his office, I was shocked as he bashed his arm against the wall to stop and turn his chair so that he could push his way into the room. That was just my first experience of his enormous courage and inner strength.

Shortly thereafter he decided to live on his own, hiring a helper to come in only to get him up in the morning and to put him to bed at night. In the between times he did his own cooking, played computer chess, read theological works voraciously, and even developed prize-winning nature photographs—all with the limitations of only bicep muscles and fingers that curl into his palms. However, in those times of caring for himself he also experienced long hours of work to pick something up, to struggle to find a way to turn a piece of meat in the frying pan, or to eat it without being capable of cutting it.

In his presentations to congregations Linden often asks the participants to try shaking hands with a neighbor while their fingers are all curled in, so that they can experience what it is like to feel people withdrawing from them. More than anyone, people like Linden can teach us about total acceptance of other persons. He knows more deeply than most theologians what it means not to discriminate on the basis of any sort of limitations.

How could our churches become better equipped (in both our facilities and our attitudes) to welcome into our communities people with physical and mental challenges? Perhaps we could invite an articulate handicapped person such as Linden to teach some classes for us. A committee could discover what barriers our facilities pose to persons with limitations; a task force could investigate the possibility of using someone to sign our worship services or the cost for devices to aid the hearing impaired. My great aunt teaches a special Sunday school class for her own retarded son and a bunch of his friends, provides transportation for them, and takes them home for Sunday dinner.

How might our churches become havens of comfort for the lonely? It seems often that bars have taken over the Christian community's job of providing companionship for those who are alone. Perhaps we can be more deliberate about inviting singles to join small-group Bible studies; couples can be more intentional to include them in family dinners and activities. Our churches could sponsor support groups for those who are sorely depressed in their loneliness. Instead of making single people feel left out, our vitally necessary emphasis on strengthening family life can be widened to stress that the family of the Christian community includes everyone in every station of life.

The possibilities are endless. Our congregations need to wrestle with their openness to the lonely and disabled and elderly and infirm and weak and troubled and poor. Let us create opportunities to support such people in their ministries of developing awareness. We can help them to know they are valued and loved in the community—not as oddball specimens, but as representatives of all of us, for, indeed, we all are handicapped in our own ways. Those who most clearly experience the effects of their handicaps— often because they are visually noticeable—can help the rest of us learn to cope with our limitations and learn the value of weakness in our faith lives.

Throughout our study of The Revelation, please keep in mind the foundations laid in these first three chapters. First, we established perspectives for working—careful attention to the historical situation in which, and the literary purposes for which, the book was written; appreciation for the book's various styles of literature; insistence on a theocentric focus. Then, we sketched these three main theological points of The Revelation: the ultimate victory of God, the opposition of the demonic powers, and the resultant struggles of the saints against evil. Third, we recognized that the best stance for this battle is an awareness of our weakness and total dependence on God's rule in our lives. Consequently, in contrast to the world, we who are God's people value both our own sufferings and the people among us who suffer in order that the whole community might learn lessons of dependence and trust.

Notes

1. See my chapters on "Nurturing Children" and "Abortion" in *Sexual Character: An Ethic of Intimacy for a Technological Society* (Grand Rapids, MI: Wm. B. Eerdmans Publishing Co., 1993), chapters 12 and 13.
2. There has not been much emphasis, however, on "liberation" for the handicapped and elderly. Though both Jean Vanier and Henri Nouwen work with and write of the mentally and emotionally handicapped, they have not developed a systematic theology of weakness. Yet, their books are to be heartily recommended for their wonderful insights into the grace of God and the gifts of the infirm. Also, especially valuable is Stanley Hauerwas's excellent collection of essays, *Suffering Presence: Theological Reflections on Medicine, the Mentally Handicapped, and the Church* (Notre Dame Press, 1986), which deals with many of the ethical issues related to the care of the mentally handicapped.

4

A Vision to Sustain Us in Suffering: The "Mysterious" Purposes of God

Please refer often to Revelation 1:1–3 and 9–11 as you study this chapter.

Several years ago, in a tragic time in my life, the personal support of the Board of "Christians Equipped for Ministry" kept me going. Under CEM I was freelancing as a writer and Bible teacher, and the board members held on to a vision of what CEM could become as we sought together to serve the Lord. They believed it for me even when I couldn't believe for myself. Grasping their vision and clinging to it gave me courage to face the difficulties that arose.

The Christians suffering under the emperor's persecution in Asia Minor direly needed a vision of God's sovereignty to sustain them. The words of The Revelation, recording the vision of the seer John, offered them the hope they needed. The introduction to the book helps us to understand the nature of the vision that we must hold to give us Joy in our weakness.

In modern times the word *apocalypse* often denotes terrifying visions of bizarre battles and, in the medieval phrase, hideous "ghosties and ghoulies and long-legged beasties and things that go bump in the night." The word conjures up images of variously colored horses ridden by ominous figures and of battles against monsters with lots of heads and horns and crowns. Sometimes there is also a picture of a radiantly beautiful new city, but usually those who write about the apocalypse focus more extensively on the lurid scenes.

The Greek text of The Revelation begins with the word *apocalypse*, which means "revelation" or "disclosure," and it occurs without the article *the*. That suggests either that this book is merely any old revelation or that it is so precisely *The* Revelation that no article is needed. Considering the subject matter of the text, we most accurately translate that opening phrase as *The* Revelation (which is why I have capitalized *The* in this book). Furthermore, notice in the text of Revelation 1:1 that this is the revelation of Jesus Christ. From this book we will learn what Jesus is like in all the fullness of his glorified lordship. That vision will fill us with hope. God gave Jesus this revelation to show the seer John what would happen so that God's people would be encouraged to trust his lordship in all their struggles.

The phrase, "The Revelation of Jesus Christ, which God gave him," reminds me of a concept expressed most clearly in the letter to the Ephesians. There the first chapter's glorious doxology exults in God's plan designed before the foundation of the world, purposed *in* Jesus Christ, the Beloved One, and made manifest to humankind *through* Jesus Christ. The Greek text uses the word *oikonomia*, which signifies God's plan or purpose in the *management* of the world. How astounding to realize that God's best plan was to use the suffering and death of Christ and the weakness of his followers for the fulfillment of his purposes, which he manifested in Christ!

Ephesians 1 also uses the word *mystery*, which means much more in the Bible than our English use of the word to name a puzzle to be solved. In its original sense, the Greek word *musterion* signified a secret that has been revealed and yet is too great to be comprehended. That word delightfully describes the plan of God—indeed, his purposes are mysterious to us. Even though he has made them known to us in his Word, they are still infinitely beyond our grasp. Though we spend our lives studying the Scriptures and seeking to know his intentions, we can never thoroughly understand the deepest designs of God.

That creates in us a truly humble attitude as we study the Scriptures. We might do the best we can to gain a clearer awareness of the meaning of the book of Revelation, but, ultimately, what God reveals to us will always remain mysterious. He is infinitely beyond us in his eternal majesty.

That is why we need Jesus Christ. He reveals the mysterious plan of God in ways accessible to human understanding. He makes things comprehensible to us because he was like us. We can relate to him as one who lived among others and had to work at developing a relationship with them. He was tired and had to sleep, hungry and had to eat, sad and had to grieve. Moreover, in relating intimately with us, he brought us into the possibility of relating intimately with God. Through him, the divine is brought down to earth in order that we might be exalted to the heavens.[1]

Indeed, the book we are studying is The Revelation of Jesus Christ—the way he made known to the people of Asia Minor the mysterious purposes of God, the things that were about to take place as they struggled to understand the meaning of a persecution that nearly destroyed their faith. Furthermore, we, too, can now learn about the mysterious lordship of Christ in the things that are about to take place for us in the 20th century. The Jesus Christ who made God's purposes known in the first century is still the same (Heb. 13:8), and still today he reveals the hidden things of God, so that we might have hope in the times of our tribulations.

Notice that once again in 1:2 the contents of this book are said to be the witness of the Word of God and the testimony of Jesus Christ. The seer John places his own name as bondservant between two references to God and to Jesus Christ in order to make doubly sure that we keep it straight. It is not his witness, his device, his artificial construction. The things that he is about to tell us are the very things of God, made available to us through the work of Jesus Christ on our behalf.

To make sure that we understand the importance of receiving this revelation as it comes to us from God himself, John continues by offering this guarantee: "Blessed the one reading and the ones hearing the words of the prophecy and heeding the things which are written in it." In other words, those who participated in the leading of worship by reading the seer's letter to the early Christians would find blessing in that action, and those who attended the worship celebration and who applied the word of prophecy to their lives in practical ways would also benefit.

Because we have never been deprived of God's Word, we 20th-century Christians in the U.S. too easily can begin to take for granted the great blessings of reading and hearing the texts of Scripture. Orthodox Christians in eastern Europe have much to teach us, because their worship services focus—with all the eagerness that scarcity produces—on the Word. Their liturgies date back to the earliest centuries of the church and include numerous passages from the Bible. They use candles, incense, icons, and processions to highlight the majesty and mystery of God. Even in the days of Soviet persecution, many Orthodox continued to celebrate the *mystery* of their faith and to read and sing the Word. Some of Alexander Solzhenitsyn's short stories mention the peaceful effect that the Russian countryside has on people because of all the churches and also tell of the continued faithfulness of Russian peasants in ceremonies and Easter processions that focus on the Scriptures.[2] Anthony Ugolnik shows the powerfully converting effect this reading of the Word had on the atheists who watched.[3]

Notice that when the seer John identifies himself he calls himself a brother and fellow participant in the tribulation. He does not write as one superior to his readers or distant from them. He understands their sufferings from the inside. He is participating in their anguish, too.

Moreover, John does not stop with the assurance that he shares in their sufferings. He says that he also shares in the kingdom and in the patience in Christ, which they are all practicing.

Let us celebrate the universal and timeless encompassing of the kingdom. What a Joy that the seer and the people to whom he writes are fellow participants in the kingdom of Christ—and so are we! Since that concept was a focus in the message and throughout the ministry of Jesus, we must understand what the word *kingdom* meant in the first century and how it relates to us in the 20th century.

There is much scholarly debate about the meaning of the word *kingdom*, the extent to which Jesus understood his role in its coming and fulfillment, and the significance of his ethics for the meanwhile before its culmination. The book of Revelation, however, simplifies these problems with its many images of his kingdom and its unabashed declaration that Jesus is God.

The word *kingdom* means, of course, the place or people over which a king reigns, but in the Bible the word emphasizes more the way in which God's kingdom affects the lives of all who engage in it. As J. I. H. McDonald stresses, "all are invited to join in the action by responding to God's incursion into their lives at the present moment of encounter, and by allowing themselves to be reoriented to God's future, the Kingdom in its fullness."[4] Christ's kingdom, then, changes all those for whom his lordship is supreme, who acknowledge that he is ruler over everything.

The Revelation constantly affirms that Jesus is indeed the Lord over the whole universe, that we can participate in his reign, even though the usurper Satan is trying desperately to convince the world that he is its ruler. Moreover, in falsely claiming that throne for himself, the Deceiver ushers in the heavenly battles that the book of Revelation describes.

When Jesus began preaching in Galilee, he announced that the kingdom of God had come. The Greek perfect verb recording that announcement means literally that in a decisive moment the kingdom came and, consequently, it remains in effect. Such a verb form underscores the truth that in his coming Jesus indeed brought the reign of God to bear on those who were present and that in his reign Jesus changed everything forever. Similarly (though negatively), the explosion of the first atomic bombs at Hiroshima and Nagasaki permanently changed the world by plunging it into the nuclear age. Now we can never totally remove the world from this age, though, thank God, the world is trying to reduce its weapons. Positively, the coming of Jesus changed the world radically, decisively, permanently. For those who believed in him, the reign of God continued to hold sway even in persecution. Now under his lordship they would choose to seek the fulfillment of his purposes in their lives.

Furthermore, when Jesus sent out the disciples to proclaim the kingdom (see, for example, Luke 9 and 10), he sent them with this message: "The kingdom of God has drawn near." Once again, the Greek perfect verb underscores the fact that in them the kingdom had been brought, and it would continue to exist wherever God's people go.

What exciting things can happen when we join in the action of God's incursions into human history and life and become reoriented to God's future—when we recognize the precious commodity we carry with us, in us, through us, wherever we go. Have you ever stopped to think that you bring the kingdom of God to your local grocery store?

One day a woman in front of me in the grocery checkout line was weeping silently. In a stumbling way I said to her something like, "Excuse me. I don't mean to meddle or anything, but you seem so sad. I wonder if there is anything I can do to help." She seized my offer eagerly, pouring out to me the troubles that weighed her down—and the kingdom of God was there. How often I wish for more such opportunities to bring God's reign to bear on local situations! I am sure there are many more openings than I see.

John's introduction reminds us that we are fellow participants in the reign of God. We bring his kingdom wherever we go. Moreover, because we are fellowsharers in it, we *together* bring it wherever we go. That can be a tremendous source of strength for each of us as we pursue our various ministries. Many faithful supporters of CEM under which I freelance assure me that they uphold my speaking engagement in prayer. That gives me courage for whatever I do in the work of the kingdom.

Once, before spending my graduate school spring break teaching in Southern Idaho, I asked the congregation in which I participated to pray for the various activities that were planned, especially as I tried to deal with some divisive problems in the churches I would be visiting. Two days after I arrived in the Boise area, a member of one of the congregations ended his life. He had been deeply discouraged by the struggles of kidney dialysis, but he always cared about others and even in his death sought to make things easier for those who attended him. The news of his death overwhelmed me with sorrow. Because of previous visits to his congregation, I cared about him deeply as a special friend, but had not yet had a chance to see him. His death seemed to be more than I could bear along with the other anxieties of the week. However, in the midst of that time of mourning, I became suddenly very aware of the supportive prayers of the congregation members back in Indiana. Past experience had taught me that when they promised to pray for me, they really did. In fact, one member had sent a note just before I left to assure me that her family was indeed praying. The whole congregation truly shared with me in the work of the kingdom.

This is one of the most important parts of the vision necessary to sustain us: a recognition of the community in which the kingdom of God is experienced. We are not alone as we seek to bring the reign of Christ to bear on the situations of our times. Just as John was there to encourage those struggling under the emperor's persecution, so we have each other to be fellow participants in both the tribulations and the kingdom as we live today.

Finally, John's trio of what he shares with the Asian Christians includes participation in their patience, *hupomone*. We will extensively study this word later in chapter 18, but now it is important to notice how these three terms work together to provide the context in which John shares his vision.

He calls himself "brother" to his readers and then exults that he is a fellow participant in their *tribulations* (which they have to undergo because they have been doing the work of the kingdom), in the *kingdom* (which makes all the suffering worthwhile), and in their *patience*, the means by which the other two elements are brought together. It is the gift of patience that enables us to keep undergoing the suffering that doing the kingdom work brings us. Just as we are encouraged by the fact that we do not ever have to suffer tribulations alone, nor do we have to work alone as we carry out our particular calling in the kingdom, even so we also have each other to increase our patience.

That is why I dedicate this book to Linden and to Tim. A dozen years ago, when I first envisioned this book, those two men, more than any others, shared with me their patience. By virtue of their steadfastness and profound trust in the Lord, I have been helped in many times of discouragement about my physical limitations. Still today the memories of past conversations encourage me when I get tired of the struggle.

One time when I was deeply frightened by crazy insulin imbalances and the seeming impossibility of maintaining good health, I cried my terror and despair over the telephone to Tim: "These blood count swings are taking years off my life." He calmly replied, "I just always try to remember that Jesus is Lord over my body, too." His gentle patience increased my own.

That is why John's words to us are so refreshing. He does not write as a distant observer. He is there in the midst of the persecution, exiled to Patmos for his witness of the Word of God and the testimony of Jesus (notice again in verse 9 the repetition of this phrase from the beginning of the book). When he reports his vision, then, we can celebrate it with him more deeply because we know that he understands our pain. We are not alone in our struggle; therefore, we can join him in the hope.

To that vision of hope we turn in the next chapter.

Notes

1. This cycle is one of the great themes of the gospel of John—as proclaimed, for example, in such passages as John 1:11–14 and 3:13–21.
2. Alexander Solzhenitsyn, *Stories and Prose Poems,* trans. Michael Glenny (New York: Farrar, Straus and Giroux, 1971).
3. Ugolnik's book, *The Illuminating Icon* (Grand Rapids, MI: Wm. B. Eerdmans Publishing Co., 1989), gives a superb introduction to the many lessons we can learn from Orthodox believers.
4. Bruce Childton and J. I. H. McDonald, *Jesus and the Ethics of the Kingdom* (Grand Rapids, MI: Wm. B. Eerdmans Publishing Co., 1987), p. 48. This is the best book I have found in response to the scholarly debates on the meaning of the kingdom image in the Bible.

5

Who Is Christ
for Our Suffering?

Please refer often to Revelation 1:4–8 as you study this chapter.

"Was Jonah really swallowed by a whale?" "And did God really create the whole world in just seven 24-hour days?" "And was there originally just one man Adam at the beginning of the world?"

These are the kinds of questions often asked by those who would deny the truth and authority of the Scriptures. They want to prove that most of the stories in the Bible are not believable and thereby to render not viable the claims of Christianity.

While we must readily acknowledge that these are good questions, it is important to stress instead that they are not the place *to start* if we want to discuss the relative merits of various faith claims. If we want to debate the authenticity of Christianity or its relevance in the 20th century, then we must begin with this central question: What do you think of the Christ?

Right at the beginning of his introduction to the book of Revelation, the seer John proclaims to us his understanding of who the Christ is and his significance for our lives. By the gift of the Holy Spirit, we Christians accept and believe what he writes. Before proceeding with this chapter, read carefully the picture he offers in Revelation 1:5–8. Several elements in this description are important for our theology and for our hope and comfort.

First of all, Jesus is called "the faithful witness." The Greek word order placing the adjective after the noun makes the point even more emphatically since he is thereby called "the witness, the faithful one." Indeed, Jesus is faithful in presenting to us what God wants to reveal about himself. What he shows us about God is guaranteed to be true. What confidence it gives us to know that we can always trust all that Jesus has demonstrated to us in his life and teaching about God! Just as Jesus never turned anyone away who came to him in need, so we know that the Father will always hear us when we come to him in prayer. Just as Jesus touched the weak with kindness and sensitivity, so we know that we, no matter how desperate, are thoroughly understood.

We know deep in our beings that anything's witness to itself ought to be true—that is why it is so frustrating whenever we are deceived. When an advertisement misleads us, and the campsite disappoints us greatly or the product does not clean our soiled laundry as it had claimed it would; when a friend who promises to stand beside us in a difficult time abandons us in a moment of crisis—in our reactions to such failures, we recognize how necessary it is for a witness to be faithful.

The seer John declares that Jesus is the faithful witness, and that is the challenge we can set before others who question the merits of Christianity. We can demonstrate from his life and death and resurrection, from his ascension and the sending of the Holy Spirit, that Jesus is who he claimed to be. We can survey the First Testament to sketch his fulfillment of God's promises for the Jewish Messiah. Jesus incarnates for us what God is like so that we can begin to grasp the infinity of his love.

Second, the seer calls Jesus "the firstborn of the dead." That is a tremendously important statement both for its facticity and for its implications. Though the facticity of the physical resurrection of Jesus is highly debated in modern theology, the burden of proof lies with those who deny it, and we who believe can boldly question their claims to demonstrate any other way to account for the evidence of the empty tomb and the long traditions of faith. Some of the implications are elucidated when Paul writes, "If Christ has not been raised, your faith is worthless; you are still in your sins" (1 Cor. 15:17 NASB). Christ's resurrection from the dead positively assures us that his work of redemption has fulfilled God's purposes, and therefore we are set free from our sins. Furthermore, his resurrection comforts us with the hope that someday we, too, shall rise (1 Cor. 15:20–22). Consequently, as we struggle with the limitations of this body and life, we can look forward with Joy to the time when those limitations will be swallowed up in death and we will receive a new body and an incorruptible existence.

Third, the seer tells us that Jesus is the one ruling with power and dignity over all the kings of the earth. What a substantial security that must have given the early Christians being persecuted by the Roman powers! Similarly, this statement has tremendous implications for us who live in an age terrorized by regional wars and economic chaos. Sometimes it seems that everything is out of control, but the fact that Christ rules over all human governments gives us a different basis for approaching political questions.

The amazing thing about the reign of Jesus Christ over all the kings of the earth is that it is coupled with love. When we think about the governments of the world, we would hardly ever think that any of its rulers love us. The idea is almost ludicrous. On the other hand, throughout the Scriptures God's reign over the world has been described uniquely as a lordship that combines his sovereignty with his infinite love.

The seer describes Christ as the one who both loves us and has released us from our sins by his blood. Not only does his love reign now in our lives, but also that love caused him to be willing to sacrifice himself to make possible our release from the demonic rule of sin.

Think of some of the great heroes of the world who have sacrificed themselves in order that others might be released. For example, Dietrich Bonhoeffer died in a prison camp because he attempted to confront the tyranny of Hitler. However, Bonhoeffer had no power; he did not rule. Rarely in the history of the world can we find anyone who possesses a profoundly sacrificial love and also reigns.

Furthermore, this loving Christ made us a kingdom and priests together with himself. Participants in his reign, we extend its sway over the world. Moreover, all believers serve as priests, ministering to others by means of his love and bringing the intercessions of the people to him.

That is why the seer reminds us that all glory and power belong to him into the ages of the ages. Once again this statement gives us a new perspective for responding to the powers of this world. If all the glory and power belong to Jesus Christ, then we have no right to give it to another ruler.

John wrote to encourage Christians who were tempted to give up their faith because of the oppressive powers of the Roman state. Similarly, in our times, we are constantly tempted to give undue authority to the powers of this world. The Revelation calls us back to the priority of Christ. Our values and choices must be directed by Jesus alone.

Indeed, the power and glory belong to Jesus "forever." The original Greek phrase literally says, "into the aeons of the aeons," which underscores not only the duration of the reign of Christ, but also its depth and scope. In contrast to the aeons of this world—its systems of practices and the standards associated with secular society—the kingdom of God invites us to find Christ's lordship in everything. Christ himself is in charge of all aeons. His reign forever stands over against the world's thinking and its cares (see, for example, Mark 4:19 and 1 Cor. 3:18). His glory will be displayed if we live according to his lordship in the midst of the world.

Next, the seer alerts us—with a strong "Behold!"—to the promise that Jesus is coming with the clouds and to the assurance that all eyes shall see him (including those of the present powers who won't want to). When Jesus announces this in the gospel of Luke, he makes very clear an important part of his timing, which has great relevance for our interpretation of The Revelation.

In Luke 21, Jesus sets up a pattern that circles twice to differentiate between signs of the times and signs of the end. In connection with both the destruction of Jerusalem and his coming at the end of time, Jesus declares that many things will happen, but that only one sign announces the end. First, he shows that persecutions and trials before the Roman and religious governments will afflict believers until finally the desolation of Jerusalem will be recognized at the time when armies lay siege to the city (Luke 21:20). In other words, they will know the end has come because it will *be* the end.

Similarly, there are many signs of the age, the times in which we live—such as wars and rumors of wars, earthquakes, disturbances in the heavens, and so forth. All these signs of the age remind us that it is an evil aeon, that the reign of God has not taken over yet in entirety. On the other hand, this will be the one and only sign of the end: the great vision of Christ coming in the clouds, which will cause every knee to bow. Till that time, Jesus warns, we are not to go chasing after those who speculate about the end (Luke 17:23 and 21:8). Instead, we are to be doing the work of the kingdom—caring for the needy, helping others to know about the kingdom and the love of God, bringing the kingdom to bear on the realities of this world. We are to remain watchful, to be prepared for the end so that its coming will not take us by surprise, but we are not to chase after it, for no one can know the time of its coming and its purposes are mysterious. No one will miss it when the time comes, however, for every eye shall see him coming in the clouds.

We must keep this context of Jesus' words in mind when we consider the meaning of The Revelation. One of the reasons that the book causes great anxiety for many people is that so many theologies try to use it to pin down the calendar, to try to ascertain exactly when these things shall take place. *However, Jesus told us specifically not to chase after such things.*

We cannot know the times or seasons for the purposes of God. Jesus declared that even he didn't know. That is not the reason for the pictures and announcements of The Revelation, as our first chapter stressed. All that we can know about Christ's Second Coming from this chapter's text is that when he comes in the clouds no one will miss him. That is all we need to know. And because we know that, we don't have to fear about the end, but we can be busy until it happens doing the work of the kingdom and being faithful to our priesthood.

One other fact that is clear about the return of Christ is that those who have rejected him will regret that choice. Our text says that those who have pierced him will beat themselves on account of him. The next phrase, "all the nations of the world," helps us to know that the passage is not referring specifically only to those who pierced Jesus on the cross, but to all those from any nation who have pierced him in rejection of his claims.

Finally, the last phrase, "Even so, Amen," which doubly emphasizes that this shall indeed come true, reminds us that the coming of Jesus will introduce a dramatic division of the world into those who have responded to his love and accepted his ruling lordship and those who continue to pierce him. Then, extra affirmation is added by the potent reminder in verse 8 of who this God is who declares these things, for the Lord God himself is the Alpha and the Omega, the beginning and the end (a concept found in such places as Is. 41:4). The idea that God was and is and is to come is also a strong image throughout the First Testament, implied in the very name Yahweh, which means "I Am." The name *Almighty* is a favorite in Genesis and Job and is suggested in the scores of uses, especially by Isaiah and Jeremiah, of the name "LORD of hosts." In contrast, the name *Almighty* is used for God only 10 times in the New Testament, but nine of those instances occur in the book of Revelation. Surely here, as nowhere else in the New Testament, the image of God as the powerful one, able to do whatever fits his purposes, is especially reinforced. This is the God who stands behind the announcement of the dividing of the world at the Second Coming of Christ. As surely as God has always been and always will be and truly now is—as surely as he is the almighty one, totally capable of accomplishing whatever he purposes—so surely can we know that when Christ comes the whole world will know it, and everyone in it will be compelled to acknowledge his lordship.

All sorts of principalities and powers do battle against that lordship (as we will see in studying other parts of The Revelation), and many times the circumstances in which we find ourselves seem to indicate anything but his lordship. That is why we need the book of Revelation—to keep reminding us of this essential perspective: the Christ is the fulfillment of all God has promised; in him the witness to God's love and power is faithfully presented; when he comes again the whole world shall recognize the truth of his claims.

6

Who Is the Son of Man?

Please refer often to Revelation 1:12–20 as you study this chapter.

The gruesome painting showed a man in brilliant white garments and a golden belt, but his hair was hoary white and belonged to someone ancient, and that was totally incongruous with his youthful, virile face. Furthermore, a huge sword coming out of his mouth destroyed any sense of reality or comeliness. The artist had obviously tried to produce an image of the Christ drawn in the introduction to the seer's vision in Revelation 1. His grotesque picture representing graphically the text illustrates well the error of interpreting the book of Revelation too literalistically.

We must distinguish between *literal* and *literalistic* interpretations in order to learn better skills for understanding The Revelation appropriately. The first term means to take the Scriptures seriously, to believe that what they say is indeed the vital Word of God, authoritative to guide our lives in truth. To interpret the Scriptures literalistically, on the other hand, is to forget that the Word of God is magnificent literature, making inspired use of symbols and metaphors and other artistic devices to underscore its messages. The book of Revelation offers many pictures that are not to be understood as "visual reality," but as true symbols signifying various dimensions of the character of God. Thus, from the picture of Christ in Revelation 1:12–20 we learn much about his character, but certainly cannot draw a portrait of him.

One of my fiercest childhood arguments with an older brother was whether Jesus was handsome. To my young mind holiness meant that he had to look perfectly elegant. When my brother insisted that Jesus probably wasn't all that spectacular, I went to bed in tears. I couldn't cope with his humanity yet.

Much later someone taught me the passages in Isaiah that portray a Suffering Servant so disfigured as to be beyond recognition and desirability. Certainly Jesus took upon himself a humanity so perfectly complete that he could suffer ugliness, deprivation, and torture as truly as any person.

The truth is that we cannot use the Scriptures to describe anything other than the character Jesus reveals to us. All these images are designed to usher us into his presence, but once there we realize that he is too glorious in his lordship for us to do anything but describe him inadequately and recognize our limitations in perceiving him. The seer uses the best images possible to convey to human minds the impressions that he experienced in his vision, but we all know that any words are going to wind up short.

This does not at all discount the fact of inspiration. Rather, it underscores the wonder that God condescended to inspire the biblical writers to convey the truth of his character in words that bring his presence to readers unable in their human and finite abilities to comprehend his transcendence.

Thus, the seer describes the Son of Man with many expressions of majesty, each of which brings to mind images and attributes revealed in the Hebrew Scriptures. The first of these is the very title "Son of Man." Occurring over 50 times in the book of Ezekiel and at a strategic spot in the book of Daniel, the term was well-known in Israelite circles, to the extent that when Jesus called himself by that name, he was greeted immediately with charges of blasphemy (see, for example, Mark 14:62–64). In Daniel 7:13–14 the Son of Man goes to the Ancient of Days and receives from him dominion and glory and a kingdom that shall not be destroyed. In ascribing this title to Jesus, then, the seer proclaims Jesus' authority of deity and the fulfillment of God's promises to restore the kingdom of Israel under the messianic rule.

Furthermore, this Son of Man is found by the seer in the midst of seven golden lampstands (the significance of which is discussed below) and dressed in the golden belt that might be expected of one so royal. His long, flowing robe reaching to his feet, however, differs from the usual short tunic worn by warriors and lords of power. His head and hair are unusual also in their brilliant whiteness—as wool and as snow. In the context of this picture such an image does not signify premature aging, but his purity and victoriousness and, undoubtedly, the wisdom and spiritual maturity that are associated with white hair in the Hebrew Scriptures. The white-ness of wool and snow reminds us of Isaiah 1:18 and comforts us with the assurance that this Son of Man is the one who forgives our scarlet sins and makes us white and pure, too.

We can understand the images of fire also because they come from Daniel 7:9–10; 10:6; and Ezekiel 1:26–27. Eyes that are flames of fire and feet that glow as bronze having been set on fire in a furnace emphasize the penetration of his vision, the strength of his power, the radiance of his majesty.

From the book of Ezekiel comes also the description of the voice like the sound of many waters, so as the listeners to John's word of encouragement in The Revelation heard that phrase they probably remembered the Hebrew context of that picture at the beginning of the prophecy about the departure of the glory of the LORD from the temple and its return when the people of Israel were restored after the Babylonian captivity. In the same way, then, first-century Christians could draw hope for their eventual deliverance from the present captivity under the Roman emperor. Similarly, we Christians in the 20th century can look for the final restoration of the people of God, though now our world is captive to the material-ism and self-centered egoism of our age. The voice of the water-falls still flows.

One element of the picture that cautions us against interpreting any of the pictures in The Revelation too literalistically is the detail of the seven stars (see below for their significance) in the Son of Man's right hand, for three verses later he puts that same right hand on the shoulder of the seer. A graphic representation of these verses would necessitate picturing the seer getting poked in the shoulder with stars. My comments here probably seem too simplistic and self-evident, but we must firmly establish these principles for a literal interpretation at the beginning of our study together so that we will not fall to the temptation later to be literalistic about such things as the 1,000-year reign of Christ or the 144,000 saints who will inhabit heaven.

Almost certainly we can associate the two-edged broad sword coming from the Son of Man's mouth with the sword of Hebrews 4:12 or Ephesians 6:17, even though the Greek texts use different words for sword (but the same word for two-edged). The image of the Word of God as a sword seems to have been "in the air" in the first century—that is, in the environment of the early pacifist Christians the figure of the Scriptures as their sword was used in contrast to the various weapons used by the Roman military.

This concept of figures of speech "in the air" is very important for our historical perspective on The Revelation. Many images used in the book are no longer accessible. Since they have fallen out of our Christian vocabulary, we cannot be sure to what they might refer. We can make educated guesses, but we are not able to know for sure whether we have correctly cracked the code. Certainly the images were clearly understood by the seer's readers, for he employed those that were utilized in the worship and conversation of early Christians so that his letter might lucidly convey the hope he intended.

Because 20 centuries have intervened, however, it is dangerous to suppose that we can know for sure to what the images refer. Our guesses must always be tentative. We certainly can't pin down various elements of these visions and assert that they are particular signs being fulfilled in our age to help us calculate the chronology of Christ's return. As emphasized in the previous chapter, the only way we will know for sure when Christ will return is when we actually see him coming in the clouds—and, since clouds always represent in the Scriptures the presence of God (see, e.g., all the references to God descending in a cloud in Exodus, Leviticus, and Numbers, and also at the transfiguration of Jesus in Matt. 17:5), that image, too, is more important as a symbol than as an actual description of how Jesus will physically come.

Once again, the Son of Man's power is underscored in the description of his face as shining as the light of the sun in its strength. This image is easy for us to grasp. We know the power of the sun in its brightness and in its ability to burn us if we stay out in it too long. No wonder the seer, upon seeing him, immediately fell to his feet as dead. Throughout the Scriptures we read of those who, confronted by the holiness and majesty of God, fall down in worship and dread. No one can face the holy God and stand, unashamed.

Imagine a whole page filled with descriptions of God—each phrase etched in a different bright color and style of calligraphy.

The words are stacked together tightly, as if to pile image upon image in a brilliant engraving of the spectacle of God's appearance. Finally, at the bottom of the page, the transition, "And when I saw it," is printed in a neutral color. Suddenly, upside down, is the response, "I fell face downward on the ground."[1] The majesty of God turns us upside down, and we fall on our face in unworthiness. It throws us to our knees in adoration and utmost humility.

This great awe and trepidation are usually accompanied in the Scriptures, however, by the invitation not to fear. Similarly, here in Revelation 1 the Son of Man reaches with his right hand (always symbolizing fellowship in the Bible) and tells the seer, "Do not be afraid." Though we deserve to be slain, though we cannot bear to face the holiness that cannot tolerate our sinfulness, yet we are invited by the pure and holy one to enjoy his presence without fear. What amazing grace! What a wonder to be welcomed in this way!

When the Son of Man continues by naming himself "the First and Last" (v. 17), his words carry tremendous import. That title has already been used in this book (v. 8) to signify the Almighty One. At that point we didn't know who was speaking since the names of God and of Jesus Christ had both occurred with about the same frequency in the earlier verses of the introduction to the book. Now, however, it is clear that the Son of Man is speaking, and in claiming to be the first and last he uses images from the Hebrew Scriptures (see previous chapter) and thereby asserts unequivocally his deity. He takes for himself the titles of Yahweh, the covenant God of Israel.

In keeping with our theme in the last chapter, this identification raises again the most important issue in all of life, this question that we can ask the world around us: what do you think of the Christ? Is he God himself—more than simply a good teacher, more than a prophet, and more than someone whom God adopted to fulfill his purposes? Is he actually both God himself incarnated in human flesh to dwell among us and yet also God who was and is and eternally is to come? Do we believe that this Word was always God, though now he takes a human form? The seer John and all the rest of the Scriptures answer yes; the early church and its persecuted believers answer yes; we boldly answer yes and invite the world around us to answer yes, too.

Next, the Son of Man fills that name, First and Last, with new meaning, for he received the dominion and glory from the Ancient of Days not by any huge manifestation of power, but by dying and then being raised to life. Thus, we can know that he holds the key of death and of Hades, for surely he has passed through their clutches and come out on the other side as victor over their purposes. Into the aeons of the aeons, therefore, he reigns as Lord over death and of life.

The divinity of this picture is constantly underscored by all the sets of threes. Throughout the Bible, even in the First Testament before the concept of Father, Son, and Holy Spirit could be comprehended, the sacred number three represented divinity. Often the number is used in songs of praise, such as the angels' song of "Holy, holy, holy" in Isaiah 6. The Aaronic blessing of Numbers 6:24–26 includes three statements of Yahweh's gifts to his people. The prophet Isaiah often uses three names for God in a series, such as his common phrase, "the LORD, your Redeemer, the Holy One of Israel" (Is. 48:17).

Then, in the New Testament, Jesus refers in various discourses to the persons of the Trinity, though no trinitarian doctrine is overtly stated. Many of the earliest formulations of the church are the products of long discussions in the attempt to understand more clearly the nature of the unity and distinction of the three persons in one Godhead (and still can anybody clearly understand the idea?). Truly it is a mystery, yet the paradox is apparent in the Scriptures that describe the various persons and yet claim the oneness of God. Thus, the number three enters into that mystery and symbolically underscores the deity of things grouped in threes. It is interesting to observe all the events in the life and teachings of Jesus, for example, that the evangelist Matthew records in sets of threes.

Here in Revelation 1 the instruction is given to the seer to write (1) all the things he has seen; (2) the things that are; and (3) the things that are about to take place after them. These three dimensions seem to correspond to the description of God who was and is and is to come by denoting the past, the present, and the future.[2]

The fact that the images in The Revelation stand for practical realities of the first-century church is made clear by the last verse of Revelation 1. After the seer receives explicit instructions to write the things he is learning, he is told overtly what the stars and the seven golden lampstands represent. Yet their definition is shrouded in mystery, because we do not know what the angels of the seven churches are. Does that name refer to angelic beings who watch over the churches in these seven cities of Asia, or does the term mean "a messenger," someone who might visit the churches to bring them words of hope and encouragement from John on Patmos? Perhaps the angels of the churches represent the local pastors in each situation. That last possibility seems very likely since each of the seven letters that immediately follow this description of the Son of Man begins with the instruction that the seer should write specific messages to the angel at each particular place. It would be tremendously comforting to the leaders of these churches to receive letters that assert that the Son of Man holds them in his right hand, the symbol always in the Scriptures for fellowship and personal relationship.

Finally, we are told that the seven golden lampstands stand for the seven churches themselves. This, too, is a vastly comforting revelation, for at the beginning of his portrait the Son of Man was depicted as standing in their midst. Various scholars recognize that these seven cities to which these letters are addressed form a circle in the order in which they are given, that they were also the postal centers for the seven regions of Asia Minor, and that they were primary centers for emperor worship. For whatever reason they were chosen, the churches in these particular cities are assured that the Son of Man stands in their midst, that he is present, right there in the area of persecution, with all the power and glory that has been described.

Just as the Christians of the first century struggled to keep their heads above water in the flooding of persecutions from imperial Rome, so in our time we face the conflicts of being Christians in a post-Christian age and need to hear again the encouraging word that the Son of Man walks in the midst of the lampstands. While we are called to be light givers in a sin-darkened world, the Son is walking among us to trim the wicks, to stir up the flames, to make our lamps more effective in transmitting his light. Indeed, the seven letters to the churches represented by those lampstands do just that as they call the churches to repentance and to new insight. In our weakness, we need to catch a clearer vision of who the Son of Man is and how his dominion and power are available in our very midst.

Notes

1. This is Timothy Botts's wonderful calligraphic rendering of the description of God in Ezekiel 1, which undoubtedly served as the source of these verses in Revelation 1. See Timothy R. Botts, *Doorposts*, 60 calligraphic renderings of Bible passages, with notes by the artist (Wheaton, IL: Tyndale House Publishers, Inc., 1986).
2. Some translations, such as TODAY'S ENGLISH VERSION, miss this symbolism entirely by using the verb *seen* as a summary and dividing it into two parts: the things the seer has seen about things that are, and the things he has seen that will soon take place.

7

Flaws and Virtues

Please refer often to Revelation 2 and 3 as you study this chapter.

"You're never going to find the perfect church." I had to keep telling myself that as I searched for a congregation in which to participate when I first moved to Vancouver. One congregation conveyed no sense of the Christian community. Another congregation had terrible music; one was not very biblically oriented. Some sanctuaries made no use at all of our rich heritage of Christian symbols. What great Joy it was finally to find a congregation that seems to balance reasonably well all the dialectics of the Christian life.

Because so many dialectical factors must be balanced in the Christian life, it is very important for us to overview the second and third chapters of The Revelation before we look at each particular letter. We need a larger picture of the whole in order to grasp the major message of these chapters.

First of all, we must clarify the meaning of the term *dialectic.* When two things seem to contradict each other, yet both are necessary to keep the proper balance in the middle, they form a dialectical tension. A prime example is the paradox that Jesus is both true God and also true man. If we overemphasize his divinity, we lose sight of the model that he provides for us of God's design for our true humanity, which was spoiled in the fall. As a truly human person he is able to understand us in our temptations and discouragements. Also, in his true humanity he could really—and not just theoretically—suffer and die for us. On the other hand, if we overemphasize the humanity of Jesus, then we deny his eternal membership in the Godhead, that he existed before the creation of the world and became incarnated (not merely adopted later into a previously existing human person) at the conception and birth of Jesus of Nazareth. Indeed, Jesus is both God and man, and, although those two facts seem to contradict each other, we must keep them both in tension in order to have the whole truth about who he is.

Similarly, when considered as a whole, in relation to one another, the seven letters to the churches in Revelation 2 and 3 show us several dialectical tensions, such as the poles of truth and love. These must be kept in balance in order for our congregations to become the kind of churches that Christ wants them to be—lovingly truthful and truthfully loving.

Furthermore, the letters follow the same basic pattern. The repetition of this pattern seven times over suggests to us the cyclical nature of the entire book of Revelation (a concept we will see repeated frequently). That cyclical orientation is underscored by the geographical locations of the seven churches, which roughly form a circle in the order in which they are given in chapters 2 and 3. Furthermore, five of the churches were in cities that lay on an important imperial trade route (Pergamum, Thyatira, Sardis, Philadelphia, and Laodicea), so they seem to serve as the focus for the whole region of Asia Minor. It seems that the seer intended his vision to be spread throughout the territory by means of these churches at the center of the communications network.

In order to practice skills of careful text reading and to overview for yourself the patterns and dialectical tensions in the letters, sketch out for yourself on a separate piece of paper the chart on p. 59. For each text, list the name of the church that is addressed, the description of the Christ who speaks to that particular church, and the praise, rebuke, challenge, and promise that he offers each one. In the following seven chapters, we will consider more carefully the interrelationships of these elements within each letter, and you can check your answers with my descriptions. For now it will be valuable before we summarize them for you to discover the contrasts and comparisons between the letters as a whole.

As you sketched out this chart, you certainly noticed many connections between the way Christ is described in a particular letter and how that church is challenged or rebuked or praised. Almost all of the descriptions of Christ in this section are taken from the composite portrait at the end of chapter 1, and now the references to the various parts of that description show us how intimately these

FLAWS AND VIRTUES

Text	Church	Descr. of Christ	Praise	Rebuke	Challenge	Promise
2:1–7						
2:8–11						
2:12–17						
2:18–29						
3:1–6						
3:7–13						
3:14–22						

words to the churches are tied to the nature of Christ and his care for the churches.

Even though most of the letters contain stern rebukes, they are intimately tied to the person of Christ, who holds their leaders in his hand and walks among them to comfort, to admonish, to praise. That would indeed be a great source of consolation for the struggling Christians of the first century. In the same way, we can find it vastly comforting that Christ is present in all his glory even when we deserve his rebuke.

In our times of physical weakness, in our handicaps and limitations, in our discouragements and various emotional hardships, we need the comfort of these seven letters in The Revelation, for, though the churches were weak and failing, Jesus walked among the lampstands. In our doubts, or lack of trust, or attempts to know today all the answers for tomorrow, Jesus is with us—as the First and Last, as the One who holds the seven stars in his hand, as the One who says, "Do not be afraid."

The idea of repentance is prominent in the seven letters to the churches. Five of the seven letters contain a call to repentance—for immorality, false teaching and losing the first love. In all these instances we recognize ourselves. When we glibly rely on ourselves—our own wisdom to figure out doctrine, our false pride as we gauge our morality, our own enthusiasm to be the focus of our love—then we need to repent.

The good news is that our failure to be the people that God would have us be does not remove us from the sphere of his care. His call to repentance is a sign of his continuing grace and the constant opportunity to come back into relationship with him. Furthermore, all the calls to repentance in these letters are followed by this summons: "Let the one having an ear listen to what the Spirit is saying to the churches." The Spirit keeps talking with us and inviting us to hear him. Repentance cleans out our ears!

While sketching in the chart you probably also noticed that some of the churches have the opposite problem of others. The church of Ephesus has lost its first love, although it won't tolerate wicked doctrine. Thyatira, on the other hand, is commended for its love and service, but rebuked for tolerating false teaching and immorality. The promises given to these churches with opposite problems are suitably appropriate—those without love are promised the tree of life (for, indeed, the return of true love will bring new life), while those with false doctrine are promised authority over the nations (which cannot be exercised when the teaching is wrong).

The combination of differences and similarities in these letters tells us something else about being churches in the 20th century. All of the churches are given a challenge, and all of them receive a promise—even those most strongly rebuked and even Laodicea, which receives no praise at all. No matter how desperate we think a situation might be in a particular congregation, God still gives his promises to that church. Grace is always present for any group of Christians, no matter how much they might be struggling.

Furthermore, even those churches that are not rebuked—notice carefully the letters to both Smyrna and Philadelphia—are still given a challenge. We dare never think that our Christian community has reached perfection. There are always certain ways in which we still must grow. We will always need to be motivated by these letters in The Revelation to stimulate our fellowship and to search for aspects of our community life and witness that are not in keeping with God's plans for his people.

The fact that each church receives a challenge and a word of promise is especially relevant for our purposes here in learning the meaning of Joy in our suffering and the importance of the weak in our Christian communities. Each church of the seven has something to offer the other churches and things to learn from the others. The churches are addressed in a circle, with the same pattern for each letter—thus, the literary form itself underscores the invitation to each to pay attention to the message for all.

No Christian community can stand alone, nor can any individual within the community think that he or she does not have to be in relationship with the rest of the body. The dialectical tensions between the letters challenge us to keep the diverse personalities of the various churches in balance. The pattern similarities keep us mindful of our unity. The references to specific parts of the picture of Christ in chapter 1 remind us that his character is what holds us all—different churches and unique individuals—together.

Finally, we must consider the phrase that is exactly repeated in every letter, "Let the one having an ear listen to what the Spirit is saying to the churches." We all are challenged to use our spiritual ears to pay attention to these letters and apply them to ourselves.

God's Word to the churches applies in any age. These letters do not project different dispensations that set up a calendar for history to unfold, until the last dispensation ushers in the final age of Christ's return. Rather, the letters are part of the whole biblical narrative that nurtures the character of the people of God. Each letter gives important warnings, and at specific times our particular churches might need them directly. At other times, to hear what the Spirit is saying helps us to know how weighty each matter is—that we regain our first love as well as maintain pure doctrine, that we persevere as well as repent.

What a shame that the book of Revelation is so often ignored or so often used for bizarre purposes! It must be understood as a book of prophecy, but to prophesy is to speak the Word of God to a particular situation (with or without implications for the future). This book of prophecy applies God's truth to each of us and to all of us together.

"Let the one having an ear listen to what the Spirit is saying to the churches." In the following chapters we will be listening to what the Spirit has to say to each of the seven churches—and to us.

8

Ephesus: Losing Our First Love

Please refer often to Revelation 2:1–7 as you study this chapter.

Sometimes putting up with physical handicaps gets so hard that the individuals who suffer begin to get terribly inward-turned. We have to focus so much on trying to take care of ourselves, and it is such a time-consuming chore, that we have no desire to help others. We lose our sense of grace and the Joy of worship. I experienced that as I worked on an earlier draft of this book; sores on my shattered foot that increased the likelihood of amputation required extra days with orthopedic specialists for multiple cast changes and adjustments. It is hard to live in loving response to God's grace when we can't understand why we have to suffer unreasonable pain and anxious distress.

This seems to have been the problem with the Christians at Ephesus. They are commended for their deeds, their work, and their patience—their ability to remain faithful in the tough situation of the emperor's persecution. They are even able, in the midst of it all, to stay strong against the false teachers—those who claimed to be apostles and yet were not, those who are described as "evil men." The Ephesians could not tolerate them. They also are commended for hating the false teaching of the Nicolaitans (to be discussed in the following chapter). Nevertheless, they had lost their first love.

How is this possible? How can they still be patiently enduring the struggles of faith, standing firm against false teachers, and involved in works of faith, and yet have lost their first love?

The lesson is especially essential for us because our personal and corporate faith lives can so easily fall into the same trap. Too often, particularly if we have been believers for quite a while, there is great danger that we will do the acts of faith without any love underneath. Marriages run into the same trouble when the outward form remains, but the inward quality of caring love is missing. To understand this problem, we must more accurately define the concept of love and look at reasons why we are likely to lose it.

First, we can clarify what problem afflicted the church at Ephesus. It was not so much that they were tired of putting up with the chore of being Christians. Nor does it seem primarily that they were weary of the struggle or that they regretted their strong stand against false doctrine. Rather, in their works of faith they had lost track of the motivation. The work was not to be loved for itself, but as a means to a greater end—as an expression of their commitment and devotion to the One who holds the seven stars.

We all run into this danger when we use our spiritual gifts. At first, in response to God's grace, we love doing what our gifts enable us to do. We know great Joy in fulfilling what we were created to do, in celebrating who we truly are, in freely serving God according to his master design. We might grow physically weary in our service, but, when love inspires us, we derive new energy and excitement from the tasks themselves.

The hazard, however, is that we might start loving our ministries for the wrong reason, envisioning the tasks as the end rather than the means. We might choose to do them because they bring us human happiness and affirmation, rather than because they are ways to respond to the God who designed them for us to do and us to do them (see Eph. 2:8–10). Then our service becomes self-centered instead of God-centered, people-pleasing rather than God-pleasing.

We cannot do eternal work if not for the sake of the eternal one. We mistake the journey for its end and love the road instead of the one who called us to walk on it.

This is an especially great danger because then our service points to the wrong focus. We do not direct others to God, but to our work, our ideas, our deeds, ourselves. The Ephesians' ability to have patience in hard times was a powerful strength, but, if its end result was patting themselves on the back for their courage, then God was not glorified.

Prime specimens of losing our first love might be studying the Sunday school lessons only for what we will teach the children or preparing devotions for how they will affect others, without first allowing the Scripture texts to confront us with their truth. We have no right to proclaim to others the transcendent power of God and how his Word changes people, unless that Word is constantly changing our lives.

The danger is especially great for professional church workers. Once, while working intensely to prepare retreat Bible studies appealing enough to counteract high school students' penchant for entertainment, I could not figure out why my plans just would not come together. The more I studied, the more restless I got, until finally I realized that I had been studying the text for the kids without first letting it speak to me. How ironic that I was working with John 15 and the declaration of Jesus that we are pruned by his Word! Immensely I needed repentance and personal pruning before my thoughts could return to the youth.

Our Christian communities need to turn to those who have retained their first love well to teach all of us the secrets of their staying power. One aspect of their faithfulness is the awareness of how precious a treasure God's love is. In the trials of life, we learn that we cannot keep ourselves, that God's love must keep us. Consequently, those whose lives have been tested have been purged of the dross, the superficial affections of lackadaisical Christians.

If they have allowed their sufferings to point them to God, those whose lives are fragile often have a deep sense of its preciousness and its giftedness. For example, our blind piano tuner also tuned my Celtic harp this year and commented on how much he enjoyed playing it. When I offered to lend it to him for awhile, he responded, "Oh, how good the Lord is to me! I've had two offers from people to let me play their harps."

Another aspect of the secret of retaining love is the discipline of nurturing it. Sometimes senior citizens or handicapped people or others who struggle with various obstacles retain their love well because the disciplines necessary to overcome their limitations also deepen their commitment.

One 92-year-old, frail but twinkly-eyed woman at a senior citizens retreat told of the trials of her life and how the Lord had safely led her through them all. Her love for God radiates from her face and in all her behavior because she has intentionally focused on his goodness to her.

We know from the analogy of marriage relationships or friendships that love can only remain strong if it is continually nurtured. During four years of long-distance friendship while I was in graduate school, my then-future husband, Myron, and I learned that in the few days when we could be together each year we needed to spend time just enjoying each other's company—going for walks to enjoy the flowers, playing baseball together, sipping tea, and talking gently. Such activities nourished our affection.

Likewise, one day while writing the first draft of this book, in my prayer before the noon meal I experienced the goodness of simply listing the blessings of the day: the home where I was staying so that I could write; the loan of a typewriter; the friendship with my hosts, which had lasted for 14 years and over great distances; God's gifts of food and time and flowers. Recounting these blessings increased my sense of gratitude and deepened my love for the Creator and Giver of every perfect gift.

The desire to retain our first love invites us to have a daily devotional period for reading the Scriptures, meditating on them, and spending time in prayer. We need such disciplines to focus our attention on who God is and how he loves us, how he has gifted us, and how his grace sustains us. As we ponder those blessings, truly our love is quickened and nourished and sustained.

The Ephesian Christians really had a lot going for them. Their continued patience in afflictions, their faithful performance of good works, and their battles against the opposition of evil persons and false doctrines tell us that they were wonderfully devout people. The fact that they nevertheless needed to be reprimanded helps us see the grave relevance of this letter. No matter how active our Christian faith, we do not serve God's best purposes if love does not motivate what we do.

The seriousness of this problem is also demonstrated by the threat to the church at Ephesus that their lampstand will be moved out of its place if they do not repent. This threat is being fulfilled in many contemporary churches that have fallen away from their first love. As they are less and less motivated by adoring commitment to their Lord, the focus of the congregation's strength begins to shift. Then folks start moving away to other churches where the love of God prevails, where Joy inspires commitment and adoration. Many mainline Protestant denominations are losing members to more on-fire churches that stress deeper discipleship and love.

On the positive side, the message to the Ephesians stresses that if they repent of this loss of love they will experience an open possibility to eat of the tree of life, which is clearly defined as the place of blessedness (the paradise) of God. If they repent and recognize their need to nurture their love for him, they will be enabled to make use of his nurturing gifts.

God so wants us to be in love with him that he makes it possible for us to be nurtured in that love. He makes his presence always available to us so that we can focus on him in adoration and praise.

To do so, however, requires discipline—not at all a favorite word in our contemporary society, which would rather do only the things that feel good. The original Greek verb (which is stronger than our English translations) criticized the Ephesians because they had *abandoned* their first love. Their desertion reminds me of the bumper sticker, "If you're not feeling close to God, guess who moved."

If we are not passionately in love with God, it is not because he has stopped blessing us. We might be going through some difficult times at the moment, but God is still the same at work in our circumstances to bring the best for us. The letter to the Ephesians invites us, when we have moved away, to repent of that movement and to receive again God's immense love for us.

Love grows when it is fed—such a simple principle but so easily forgotten. Love dies from malnourishment—so major a problem that the letter warning of its danger comes first in the set of seven. Here we must start in learning the meaning of The Revelation: with an honest assessment of our lack of love and an open confession of our failure to accept God's grace and forgiveness. Let us clearly recognize that God will produce in us the love for him that must be the foundation of our faith lives if we let him have the time to create it in us.

In our busy world, we rarely give him the time. Thus, one of my goals in this book is that our study together of the lessons of The Revelation might usher us into the Lord's presence, so that our love for him might be nurtured.

9

Smyrna: Limitations
of Suffering

Please refer often to Revelation 2:8–11 as you study this chapter.

I love to sing the great hymn of the Reformation, "A Mighty Fortress Is Our God." Its lines reverberate with the triumph of God over "the cruel oppressor" and all the "craft and dreadful might" of the powers of evil that "threaten to devour us." What glorious assurance that "God's Word forever shall abide," that "God himself fights by our side with weapons of the Spirit," and that "the Kingdom's ours forever!" How comforting to know that we don't have to be the ones who overcome by our own efforts! Instead, our hearts soar with the realization of the tremendous hope we have in God. The Lamb who was slain for us has already overcome all evil and weakness (see chapters 30–31 below), and someday all believers will fully participate in his victory.

It is crucial that we deliberately note near the beginning of this book that a theology of weakness does not preclude eventual triumph. The assurance of ultimate victory and an understanding of weakness work together to give us courage for facing the meanwhile time (see the following chapter). Our desire to learn biblical patience is founded on the assurance of our eventual participation in the triumph of the slain Lamb.

The letter to Smyrna, which is the subject of this chapter, is the only one of the seven that does not have any warning or negative criticism of the church. Because of their sufferings the Spirit has only words of encouragement for the members of this community. We cannot blithely read these words without acknowledging our failures and need for repentance, but the words of comfort are yet richly available to us in the 20th century.

Seven phrases of the message to Smyrna give us hope and comfort for our times. The first is that in our tribulations and poverty we actually are rich. The letter does not say specifically in what that richness lies, but in context with the rest of The Revelation and with all of the Scriptures we can easily suggest several good possibilities. We are rich, obviously, in our relationship with the Lord and in the gifts he showers on us. We are rich, furthermore, in our relationship with the community of his people and in the support for our tribulations that the community provides. Moreover, our wealth is founded on the assurance that these tribulations are not God's last word to us. Rather, the promises of this letter can carry us through them.

Second, the Spirit assures the people of Smyrna that he knows about the slander they are receiving from those who claim to be Jews, but actually are "a synagogue of Satan." We don't know specifically to what situation these words refer, but again we can make some educated conjectures. When the earliest Christians proclaimed Jesus as the fulfillment of the Hebrew prophecies, they specifically encountered opposition from the so-called Judaizers, who acknowledged Jesus as the Messiah, the Christ, but demanded that Jewish ritual obligations be imposed on new Gentile converts. Indeed, their demand denied Jesus' message that salvation comes by means of the grace of God and not by fulfilling religious obligations. (See Paul's diatribes against this heresy in Gal. 1–3.) This work of Satan continues in our time whenever the message of grace is lost in efforts and works. The Spirit comforts the Smyrna church by declaring that God understands the blasphemy against them.

We must put such a text carefully into its historical context to prevent it from being mistakenly perceived as anti-Semitic. Revelation 2:9 is not slander against a people or against their ethnic heritage—indeed, it was written by a Jew primarily for Jews. Rather, the verse cautions those who claim to be God's people, but in reality deny his purposes. We must pay attention to the warning because we can easily appear on the surface to be Christians and yet, by our legalism and failure to forgive, reject the grace of Christ.

Next, the people at Smyrna are urged not to fear what they are about to suffer. This comment becomes especially valuable when we consider their situation of intense suffering in the persecutions of the Roman emperor. Certainly we would all greatly fear what might have to be undergone in the future. However, the Spirit's words remind us that fear about what we might experience does not really help us endure the suffering. Rather, our fear usually does the reverse—it makes the suffering more difficult to bear.

Fear increases both physical pain and psychosomatic agony. Most of the things we spend time dreading turn out to be harder because of that panic.

At first when I shattered my foot, alarm about the probability of amputation prevented me from thinking of ways to cope with the daily difficulties. Only after 10 days of traveling and teaching did I begin to trust that other people and ingenuity would help me get around all right and that God would use me for his work anyway. When I panic about the unknowns of the future, I need to remember those lessons in trust.

The invitation in verse 10 not to be afraid, however, involves more than simply a recognition that fear does not really help us deal with sufferings in our lives. Even more important is the underlying basis for trust, which is given by all the reasons for hope in the rest of the letter to Smyrna.

Several dimensions of verse 10 itself underscore the truth that for no reason do we have to fear. The sentence begins with a word that accentuates the meaning of *nothing*. It says intensely, "In no way." Then the imperative *to fear* is in the present tense to stress continuation. Thus, the phrase literally declares, "Under no circumstances do we need to be fearing" that which we are suffering (also a present continuing infinitive). This combination of verb forms underscores the present action—we are about to be suffering many things, but, in the process of it all, for no reason do we need to be fearing.

The first reason not to fear is that the suffering is limited to 10 days. The number 10 in the Scriptures always symbolizes completion. The 10 basic commandments cover all the important dimensions of life. Tens of tens of tens (a thousand) always stands for the complete number of years—that Christ will reign for a thousand years means that his reign will be divinely fulfilled. The promise of only 10 days, then, limits the suffering to only that which is necessary to accomplish the purposes of God. Satan might throw us into prison, and in the process we will certainly be tested, but we will not be tested above what we can bear and, when it is sufficient, the tribulation will be over.

When I was in graduate school, a visiting Jewish philosopher lectured on God's testing of Abraham. He recounted a midrash (interpretive story) told by Jewish rabbis to explain the odd situation of God asking Abraham to sacrifice his only son, Isaac. According to the midrash,

> Abraham said to God: "Why did I have to undergo this experience? Did *you* need a test to determine my faithfulness?"
>
> And God answered, "No, I didn't need a test."
>
> Then Abraham said, "Did *I* need a test to prove my own faithfulness?"
>
> And once again God answered, "No."
>
> "Then why did I have to go through this experience?" Abraham asked.
>
> "As a witness to the nations," God replied.

This answer offers tremendous comfort when we are plagued by the endless "Why?" questions. We don't know why God allowed Satan to throw the people of Smyrna into prison, nor why we might have to suffer in various ways. Recently I went through a seven-month period of near-blindness because of retinal hemorrhaging and of crutches and wheelchairs because of wounded feet. Searching for meaning in that incapacity, which started just two weeks after receiving my Ph.D., I was prodded to faithfulness by this hope that God uses even our times of trial for his purposes. The faithfulness of the people of Smyrna recorded in The Revelation still stands as a proof to the world of God's love and care, as a witness to the nations that Jesus is Lord.

This is a substantial hope for our times of trials. Those around us who wonder about God might observe our response to suffering and then judge accordingly. Our attitudes in suffering can be powerful vehicles for evangelism.

Long ago when I taught "Literature of the Bible" in the English department at the University of Idaho, some of my colleagues enjoyed making fun of my faith and giving me hassles in the department. One of my students came to see me right after I had received particularly bad news about a department matter. I had been crying from the frustration of it all, and yet God had given a great sense of peace that he would bring something good out of that situation. Later that same student told me that my reaction in that difficulty was one of several factors leading to his recognition of the truth of Christianity. We can, indeed, be encouraged not to fear in the midst of times of tribulation not only because we know that the struggles are limited to 10 days, but also because we know that they can be vehicles of proof to those questioning the reality of Christ and the truth of the Gospel.

The next reason that we need not be fearful in times of suffering is that we have this promise: if we continue to be faithful unto death, the Lord will graciously give us the crown of life. The adverb *graciously* must be stressed there because the Greek text uses a word that emphasizes such giving. God does not *have* to give us the crown of life as a reward for our faithfulness. Even though we might go through many trials and remain thoroughly faithful in them all, we still couldn't deserve the gift of his crown. His giving it to us in spite of our inadequacy is utterly the product of his grace. Knowing, then, that the gift is ours—not by virtue of *our* success in remaining faithful, but because of *God's*—gives us the assurance to keep carrying on. We are released from the pressure that if we fail we will lose everything. Rather, we know that we have everything to gain, and, therefore, we can have courage to keep trying to be faithful in all the tribulations of our lives.

A two-mile community run gave me the best illustrations of that motivation. Because all the participants of a retreat I was leading were entering, I joined them in the Columbia River Run 10 years ago. At that time already I could not run well because of health problems, so I knew before I even started that I would come in last—and, sure enough, I did. However, what makes such a run fun is that no matter when we finish people cheer us on because we *are* finishing. Now when I wear the T-shirt from that event, no one knows that I came in last. I did, indeed, come in.

In God's kingdom what is important is that we stay in the running, that we don't give up on the tasks. If we give up and reject the kingdom's truths as not worth striving for, God won't cram the crown of life down our throats. However, as long as we participate, as long as we remain in the running, then we are assured of the crown, no matter how poorly we finish.

This doctrine must be distinguished from heresies on both sides. It does not proclaim a once-saved-always-saved theology that allows us to slough off with a "I like to sin / God likes to forgive / isn't that a nice arrangement?" attitude. Nor, on the other side, do we perpetually have to worry whether or not the crown of life can be ours and if we have been good enough to earn it.

The necessary balance is found in the contrast of "Be faithful . . ." and "I will give . . ." On the one hand, we are called to continual participation in the work of the kingdom. On the other hand, at the same time, we keep in dialectical tension the fact that we cannot earn the crown of life at all. It is purely a gift of God's grace, never to be deserved or earned or repaid.

Finally, after the recurring invitation to hear what the Spirit says to the churches, the believers at Smyrna receive another promise: the ones who overcome in this time of tribulation shall never be injured by the second death. Have you seen the button that proclaims, "Born once, die twice. Born twice, die once"? This assurance gives us the ability not to fear in times of tribulation: if we are born both physically and spiritually, we do not have to fear the second, or spiritual, death. Physical death won't be a source of worry for us because we already possess eternal life.

Undoubtedly, this passage means so much to me because I have come close to death a few times. Even as my life becomes more and more fragile, I realize that physical death is merely a door through the last barrier between us and God. Throughout our lives we confront various barriers that separate us from God, which we go around or cross over or smash down. Finally, when we come to the point of death, only one obstacle remains—the confinements of this earthly, mortal body. When we pass through that last door, we are set free from all the limitations that kept us from seeing God face-to-face.

I originally wrote this chapter just after leading Bible studies on The Revelation for a senior citizens retreat in Iowa. I remember vividly the glow on the faces of those folk—a few of them in their 90s—as we studied passages describing what heaven will be like. Their radiance demonstrated how eager they were for the last door.

They were more than ready to conquer that last barrier that kept them from God and to enter into a life of total, perfect relationship with him. For this reason they could describe with great courage various physical afflictions through which they were passing. Their descriptions and hopes greatly encouraged the young staff people at camp.

Perhaps our congregations could invite such radiant senior citizens to speak to our youth groups or Sunday school classes about their hope for the crown of life. Perhaps in the children's messages of worship services or in visiting those who are ill in the hospital they could share with others in the community how they have learned, through many years of faithfulness, to look at death without fear and to wait for the crown of life with Joy.

10

Pergamum: The Importance of the Word

Please refer often to Revelation 2:12–17 as you study this chapter.

I had given my college roommate a secret name. Only she knew it, and I used it for her only in certain circumstances. One day we were chatting with our choir director in his office, and my roommate was complaining that life was just too much of a struggle. I simply said her special name, and her entire countenance changed. In the midst of her despair she knew that she was loved.

The letter to Pergamum ends with the promise of a new name, known only by the one to whom it is given. Seer John writes to the angel of the church that when the believers there have repented and overcome their temptations, they will receive this special signification of their new relationship with God. The vital key is heightened recognition of the importance of the Word.

No matter how frustrated I might be by physical struggles, as soon as I truly enter into personal devotional study or start teaching a Bible study, I forget the pain, the inconvenience, and the exasperation in the Joy of hearing God's Word. His Word overcomes the pains of life.

The Word of God was precisely what the members of the Christian community at Pergamum needed. It is exactly what contemporary society needs, though few would acknowledge that.

This letter describes Christ as the one who has a sharp, two-edged sword. We have previously discussed the notion that this image for God's Word was probably "in the air"—language floating around in the early Christian environment. Both Hebrews 4:12 and Ephesians 6:17 characterize the Word of God as a sword. Moreover, the first-century Christians certainly understood Christ as both bearing the Word and being the Word. The image is a favorite for the gospel-writer John, for his account of Christ's life begins with the wonderful poem about the *logos*, the Greek word for "word." That thoroughly cosmopolitan poem brings together Greek philosophical connotations of the *logos* with the Hebrew faith understanding that God's Word bears within itself the power to bring about its own fulfillment.

As we have noted in previous chapters, the description of Christ that begins each of the letters to the seven churches connects integrally with the specific message that a particular church receives. Here the connection is quite obvious. God's people can keep living righteously right where Satan has his throne only by continual participation in the Word.

The letter praises the saints at Pergamum because they have remained true and have not denied their faith in Christ, even though they have been threatened by the death of one of their greatest witnesses. We do not know historically who Antipas was, but his martyrdom could have caused much fear and consequent backsliding—and to the praise of the Pergamumians, it did not. He was killed right in their own city—therefore, the letter repeats that, indeed, this is the place where Satan lives.

We must carefully consider this repetition about the presence of Satan. We will also find in it an important message of encouragement for us in whatever struggles we might be encountering.

Where does Satan live? What gives him a throne? Pergamum provided a throne because it was the center of emperor worship in Asia Minor in the first century.[1] I hope to develop my doctoral dissertation on "The Principalities and Powers" into a future book to explicate more thoroughly the ways in which the demonic forces function in the 20th century. Their influence manifests itself in many aspects of our culture, such as politics, economics, personal and international relationships, institutions (even the churches), and technological developments.

We must be extremely careful here not to fall into an overly simplistic notion that all evil is caused by some sort of little demons (even if we don't picture them with red suits and horns and flying around with pitchforks!). On the other hand, we must not over-intellectualize the whole matter and define Satan merely as the evil deeds of human beings.

The biblical picture takes a position between these two extremes but emphasizes the supernatural element. There are definitely powers of evil external to ourselves, but usually they make use of our own humanly sinful inclinations. No one can rightly say, "The devil made me do it." The powers of evil certainly are constantly tempting us, but our own failure of will is to blame if we give in to their temptations.

However, in certain particular situations demonic influences more easily take control, and we must walk very carefully if we are called to go into them. I respect highly Senator Mark Hatfield, who writes very openly in his book *Between a Rock and a Hard Place* about the easy temptations of power in high governmental positions. Our nation immensely needs Christians in politics, but anyone who chooses to enter the higher echelons of power will probably discover there the throne of Satan.

And what about you? Perhaps you work in a place where everybody curses or cheats or is involved in sexual immorality. Or maybe the demonic influence is much more subtle—perhaps in the power plays co-workers use to manipulate each other. It is difficult to maintain one's Christian witness in a demonic atmosphere.

Similarly, those challenged physically or mentally often encounter difficulty as they try to keep clinging to Christ in the constant discouragement of worsening handicaps. Illness and disability are certainly not God's intention for human life, so we might also say that in our afflictions we can also recognize Satan's dominion.

Yet the people of Pergamum are praised. They have remained true in their circumstances. They have clung to the name of Christ, by whose power the thrones of Satan have already been cast down. Their faithfulness provides a model of the ability to continue in circumstances largely overwhelmed by the powers of evil. The name of Christ enables his people to be true.

However, the seer also criticizes some of the Pergamumians for their failure to stay true to *all* the teachings of Christ. He calls their backsliding a turning to the teachings of Balaam and the Nicolaitans. Both names give us important information.

Balaam, under contract to the king of Moab (Balak), tried unsuccessfully to curse the Israelites (Num. 22–24; see also 2 Peter 2:15–16). When that didn't work, the Moabite women led the Israelites away from God through eating food sacrificed to idols (which compromised their faith) and through sexual immorality. However, we find out later (Num. 31:16) that Balaam actually was the one who "kept teaching" (planned and led) the program under Balak. Though this was but one episode from Moab's continual pressure to turn God's people away from him, it becomes here in Revelation 2:14 (and Jude 11) representative of all such apostasy and false teaching.

The powers of evil know that they cannot conquer us through direct confrontation, even as Balaam could not curse the Israelites. Therefore, the powers of evil come to us more subtly and lead us astray by small increments.

In the first century, sexual immorality was an accepted part of much of society (v. 14), as was the purchase and eating of food previously sacrificed to idols. Although this meat from temples was often the only meat available, eating it became a touchy issue in the Christian community because it involved compromise of a believer's witness (see Acts 15:20, 29 and 1 Cor. 8).

In the 20th century, the first sin of sexual immorality very obviously is as rampant as in the first and needs to be more thoroughly addressed by the church.[2] However, how does the problem of food sacrificed to idols apply to our time?

It seems to me that many aspects of our culture involve the same material entanglement in the practices of idolatry. For example, many youth refuse to buy tapes and records from rock groups that have obvious cultic connections and thereby refuse to support their practices and influence. The principle here can be seen also in the gods of power and wealth. For example, some Christians boycott certain pineapple companies because they have bulldozed the farms of poor peasants in Latin America and made them merely seasonal laborers in order to raise pineapple for the rich in the U.S. Meanwhile, the laborers' children are malnourished because the peasants no longer can grow subsistence crops on the land now added to the fields of the wealthy. Similarly, some Christians have organized boycotts of major corporations that construct weapons systems and are industry leaders in lobbying for more and more tax money to build an ever-growing arsenal of nuclear weapons.

All kinds of economic and political questions are involved in practical application of this warning to Pergamum. For example, where do we invest our money? Are the agencies using those funds to finance the construction of weapons of annihilation? Perhaps we might want to invest in alternative agencies, such as money markets that were established to invest funds in programs that build economic stability in poorer countries. Or we can choose to place our savings in such Christian agencies as Dwelling House Savings and Loan, which finances loans for the primarily black poor of Pittsburgh and follows up with counseling and support, or Jubilee Housing, Inc., which was begun by members of the Church of the Saviour in Washington, D.C., to renovate apartment buildings for the poor.[3]

Living intentionally requires great deliberation, choosing our actions carefully so that they do not contribute to the various idolatries of power and wealth in our culture. Of course, we cannot always be successful since so many aspects of life are out of our control. However, my main goal here is simply to challenge our thinking, to invite us to live with more deliberation, to question ways in which our "eating of meat" (any economic aspect) might be related to idols (of any sort). Nationalism, militarism, other ideologies, accumulation of possessions, intellectualism, even simplicity for its own sake can all become idolatrous.

The name of Balaam is also linked to leading the children of Israel into sexual immorality, and that seems to be the case also with the Nicolaitans. Since that is such a large topic, which appears also in the following letter of The Revelation, we will reserve discussion of it until the next chapter.

We must note essentially at this point that the people at Pergamum are called to repent for these sins. Our society explains them instead. We can rationalize most of our sins—they are due to bad environment, to a failure in upbringing, to inadequate love in the home. The Word of God simply says to repent. This is a major message for our times, too, that few want to hear.

God's message leads again to the theme that underlies this book. A great gift that we can bring to the Christian community out of our weakness is a deeper sense of repentance. When we suffer and struggle to survive or if we spend long hours lying on a bed of pain, usually we are brought more in touch with our sin and the need for repentance than when we are strong and think we can figure everything out and accomplish it all by ourselves.

One reason that meetings of Alcoholics Anonymous have been so successful is that those involved repent publicly. Each individual declares to the rest that she or he is an alcoholic, wanting to change, but an alcoholic nonetheless. In frankly admitting our failures we can begin the process of change.

In a world swarming with various idolatries, we need this simple call: Repent! In my times of greatest weakness, God invariably puts me in touch with my sinfulness—not to destroy me, but to begin to heal other parts of me besides my body. Moreover, we all know the intimate connection of spirit, soul, and body. Often repentance clears the way for restoration of the body.

The community at Pergamum is warned that if they don't repent Christ will fight against them with the sword in his mouth. His Word will slay them in their sinfulness.

This does not at all mean that Christ will destroy the sinners, for immediately after the threat of his fighting them with that sword in his mouth comes the warning to listen to what the Spirit says to the churches, and that is followed by a particular promise for the saints at Pergamum. Christ never gives up on us, even if we are thoroughly involved in sin. He visits us with his Word in order to draw us back from sin, to call us to repentance, to enable us to listen to what the Spirit is saying.

The promise given to this community is singularly appropriate. If they will give up eating the food of idols, they will be given the hidden manna. Again we see close connections with the gospel of John and with the Hebrew Scriptures. In John 6, after the incident of the feeding of the 5,000, Jesus challenges the Jews not to work for food that perishes (v. 27, reminiscent of Is. 55:2) and calls himself the bread of life who comes down from heaven (vv. 33–35, 48–51). He invites people to eat of himself (v. 51), but some are offended and draw back at that point. Here in The Revelation, the people of Pergamum are offered the true food, which is the Word of God, even as Deuteronomy 8:3 reminded the people that they could not live by bread alone but by the words that proceed from the mouth of God (see also Matt. 4:4 and Luke 4:4).

The triple connections between the First Testament, the gospels, and other parts of the New Testament are important. These themes weave throughout the Scriptures: we dare not get too caught up in the material things of the world and lose sight of the need for our spirits and souls to be nourished by the food of the Word. Yet what a promise is given to Pergamum! In our repentance, we will receive that which is truly nourishing. Again we are reminded of Isaiah 55:2 (NASB), where the Lord challenges the Israelites in this way:

Why do you spend money for what is not bread,
    And your wages for what does not satisfy?
Listen carefully to Me, and eat what is good,
    And delight yourself in abundance.

This is the best food around! Why do we seek so intently for what does not satisfy? Why do we chase after the world's idols? God wants to satisfy us with the only true manna, his Word. In his grace he has made it readily available for us.

The other promise given to the people at Pergamum is indeed intriguing. To the one overcoming his or her sin (by means of repentance) Christ promises a white stone with a new name written on it, a secret name known only by the one who receives it.

The story at the beginning of this chapter illustrates the importance of a new name, symbolizing our new and graced relationship with God. Perhaps its being written on a white stone signifies its impermeability, its purity, its strength and sacredness as a covenant. The image denotes a special gift, even as the name itself signals a special relationship made possible by repentance.

The call to repentance is issued to us today. We cannot leave this letter without asking ourselves these searching questions: Of what idolatries do I need to repent? In what areas of my life do I need the cleansing/pruning of the Word of God? The hidden manna of the Word will enable us to remain true to his name and to live by our new name.

Notes

1. M. Robert Mulholland, Jr., *Invitation to a Journey: A Road Map for Spiritual Formation,* (Downers Grove, IL: InterVarsity Press, 1993) P. 163.

2. See Marva J. Dawn, *Sexual Character: An Ethic of Intimacy for a Technological Society* (Eerdmans, 1993).

3. These two agencies are decisively Christian in their approach: Dwelling House Savings and Loan, 501 Herron Ave., Pittsburgh, PA 15219-4696 and Jubilee Housing, Inc., 1750 Columbia Rd. N.W., Washington, DC 20009. Some examples of alternative money markets are Pax World Fund, P.O. Box 4395, Boston, MA 02211-4395; and Working Assets, P.O. Box 5420, Indianapolis, IN 46255-5420. Information about boycotts as described in the previous paragraphs can be obtained from INFACT, 256 Hanover Street, 3d Floor, Boston, MA 02113.

11

Thyatira: True Authority

Please refer often to Revelation 2:18–29 as you study this chapter.

Numbers 24:17 prophesies that a star shall rise out of Jacob and a scepter out of Israel—a prophecy usually understood in our New Testament times as foretelling the coming of Jesus, the Christ. Most interestingly, the image comes from the mouth of Balaam, to whom the seer John referred in the previous letter of The Revelation.

Later in Revelation 22:16 Jesus names himself "the Root and the Offspring of David, and the bright Morning Star." Consequently, when the Christian community at Thyatira is promised that Christ will give the overcomers there the morning star, we understand that to mean that he will give them the gift of himself, his very own presence in their lives.

This name for Jesus is especially beautiful. Since my metabolism deficiencies make mornings difficult, I rarely arise before the sun, but when I have to fly to the Midwest from the West Coast for a speaking engagement, I sometimes notice the morning star. At those times it brings great comfort to me because its sparkling beauty overcomes the bleakness of early-morning flights.

Those who suffer sleepless nights because of their pain often say that they, too, rejoice greatly at the morning star. It promises that soon the day will appear and the night of anguish will be over.

Jesus is the bright Morning Star. Only this letter to Thyatira offers to a church such a particular promise of the presence of Christ. However, also only this particular letter attaches the additional words "and does my will unto the end" to the constant phrase in all seven letters, "To the one overcoming . . ." The presence of Jesus is integrally connected with the doing of his will.

We must clear up one false notion right away. The connection does *not* turn faith into an effort of works to create our own righteousness. We are not warned by this letter that we earn the presence of Jesus by being good.

Rather, the combination reminds us again that Christ's constant presence is missed by us if our faith does not change the practical dimensions of life. We do not know his Spirit at work in us if we reject his lifestyle. We fail to appreciate his loving presence if we are controlled by other gods.

On the other hand, when we are doing God's will, we experience the intimate connection that is possible with Jesus. We sense his presence in us. We live *in Christ*. One Christmas a former student of mine and his wife wrote that they were newly learning what it means to be "in Christ." The phrase can be just nice words until we discover that Christ really wants to be present in every aspect of our daily lives. What an incredibly wonderful promise!

We miss it, however, if we insist on our own immoral and idolatrous choices. Every time we turn to other gods, we move away from his presence. Every time we commit deeds contrary to his will, they widen our alienation.

The very gravity of what we often consider "playing around" is underscored by the sharp contrast between the praise of the people at Thyatira and the image of Christ at the beginning of their letter. Here alone he is specifically called the "Son of God" to emphasize his divinity, and his power to command their repentance is stressed with the picture of his eyes "like blazing fire" and his feet of "burnished bronze."

The praise given to this church is noteworthy: they are commended for their deeds, their love and faith, their service and perseverance, and for the fact that they are now doing more than they did at first. What a wonderful list! However, those extraordinary accomplishments do not matter if the grand successes are marred by idolatries and immoralities.

That contrast is crucially important in the 20th century. We excuse various sins if a person is faithful in attendance at worship. We let ourselves succumb to various idolatries and excuse them because we are pretty decent Christians, doing nice things and being very loving toward our neighbors. We don't take seriously enough how much one little sin mars the whole.

Certainly there is no place for self-righteousness. Indeed, all of us fail in one point at least. I am sure we could each easily name several points at which we fail.

We are not perfect. That is why we need grace.

We dare not misinterpret this letter. Its strong warning does not mean that the Thyatirans are a lost cause. Similar to the previous letter, this one is intended to draw its recipients back to grace, to call them to repentance—and forgiveness.

The problems of the people at Thyatira are the same as those of the folks at Pergamum—idolatry and immorality—but here there is a greater emphasis on the latter, so we will concentrate on it. Please refer, however, to the previous chapter to remember the many kinds of idolatry that afflict us.

This time the warning is more urgent. The blazing eyes, the name "Son of God," the warrior feet—these images all portray more wrath concerning Thyatira than Pergamum because in this case the people have been called to repentance already, but they have refused.

The letter declares that the people will be cast on a bed of suffering and made to suffer intensely for their adultery. We dare not falsely universalize these statements. They do not mean that everyone cast on a bed of suffering has committed adultery. One of the worst griefs that we who are handicapped suffer is the frequent "witness" of others that we must be suffering because of unconfessed sins.

The image here is profoundly appropriate: those who have violated God's plan in bed will there also find suffering, and their children, the product of their activities in bed, will be killed. Such harsh statements are meant to underscore the seriousness of the sin. We certainly see its fulfillment in the 20th century when many babies conceived in fornication are aborted.

Twentieth-century churches have backpedaled on this matter, often afraid to call a spade a spade. We euphemize various sins as "sleeping together" or "playing around" or living "an alternative lifestyle" instead of truly naming them adultery and fornication. The term "single parent families" is often used to hide the fact that some of the children were born out of wedlock or have suffered the trauma of divorce. So many situations specifically violate God's design for the committed, permanent, covenantal relationship in which loving sexual union is to take place.

Single people frequently tell me, however, that remaining celibate in this world is too terribly hard—and certainly it is. For many years I too struggled with my own sexual needs as a single person.

People who must struggle for their life and movement know better than most how to discipline their bodies and wills. In an age when most people go by the philosophy "if it feels good, do it," the disabled much more wisely know how empty that philosophy is. They understand that immediate good feelings often bring lasting negative consequences. They know the importance of maintaining discipline in the care of one's body.

Of course, I am not saying that all physically challenged people are more sexually pure than their healthy peers, but I am stressing our world's desperate need for lessons of discipline, for self-controlling acts of the will over emotions. Those whose very lives depend on medical procedures strictly followed (in spite of feelings) are the best teachers of careful discipline.

Elizabeth O'Connor says in her book *Cry Pain, Cry Hope* that the concern of someone who is ill with his or her own illness is not as self-centered as that might seem, for, in a time of sickness, the illness *is* one's work.[1] That insight is extremely encouraging to me as I struggle daily with difficulties of exercising, with multiple blood tests and insulin injections, with extra precautions because of various deteriorations. All the disciplines my health problems require are part of my work, and they teach me vital insights about the superiority of will over feelings. Those tempted to immorality must counteract the sexual urges with decisive acts of will that supersede emotions.

The lesson about wholesome sexuality was taught me by Linden, my friend who is quadriplegic. Before his marriage, he lamented to me once that he was thoroughly sick of being treated as if he were asexual just because he could not demonstrate his masculinity genitally. I had never thought about that before; I had always loved him as a dear *male* friend, sensitive and very strong, even though seated in a chair. He awoke me to a large dimension of the suffering of the disabled—the opinions of others concerning their sexuality.

As Linden explored that topic with me, he enunciated many ways that he expressed his masculinity, his social sexuality. His descriptions articulated the profound character of his manhood, and his lessons helped me learn more about expressing my own femininity in social, not genital, ways.

If our churches would more thoroughly support youth in expressing their social sexuality (by being family, friends, and colleagues to them), we could spare many of them the ravages of a genital sexuality that is unprotected because it is outside the bonds of a covenant, permanent relationship. How desperately our youth need some encouragement for sexual purity in this age of "free" licentiousness. More than anything for youth in our Christian communities I crave better education and support for positive, godly sexuality.[2]

The Son of God says he will cause affliction in order that the churches might know that he is the one who searches minds and hearts. In the Bible the word *heart* never refers merely to feelings. Rather, the word conveys the idea of deliberate will, of careful intentions. God does not accept the excuse that we were led into sexual temptation by our feelings. Instead, he searches for the will that would project itself over feelings and act on the basis of what the mind knows about the commands of God against committing adultery.

Though God warns those who refuse to repent, he has a precise word of encouragement for those steadfastly trying to remain pure. He urges them simply to keep holding on to what they have—their faith and love, their perseverance, their good deeds and service, their deliberate will and mind to stay away from the idolatry and immorality of their brothers and sisters.

Hang on till I come, Jesus says. Perhaps many times you and I have hung on till someone came to relieve us on a work shift, or to help us cope with the leaking sink and screaming kids, or to assist us in walking up stairs when that task was proving impossible. These experiences teach us that a strong way to resist temptation is to keep reminding ourselves that Jesus is coming.

He is coming some day to end temptation and evil forever. We certainly want to be among his people when he comes.

Furthermore, he is coming now to aid us with his power in the fight against temptation. Perhaps he is coming in the person of a friend who will stand by us with strength for the fight. He is coming perhaps now in music or beauty to uplift us and sustain us. He came to me just now in the call of a fellow member of St. John Lutheran Church who said he would take me to the doctor today in the emergency of a new wound inside the brace on my leg.

How does he come to you? How remarkable that he comes to each of us in ways appropriate to our particular loves! One day I was immensely cheered and strengthened just by seeing something pink (though I don't even recall what it was) because that liturgical color for Joy always makes me glad.

Our Christian lives are a matter of holding on till he comes. If we persist in abiding in his will, he will give us authority over the nations.

This promise is especially important as our world becomes smaller and smaller—more and more linked by telecommunications and by economic and ecological necessities. However, we must not think that the United States presently demonstrates a Christian lifestyle that abides in God's will and, consequently, reaches out to the rest of the world with godly authority. Especially after the fall of communism, many claim a moral superiority for the U.S., but we Christians must seriously recognize that the U.S. is not respected by most other nations. We have no moral credibility.

The U.S. has often been imperialistic instead of fostering the well-being of nations. We have robbed the third world instead of promoting its economic growth. Some of our tourists act boorish, thinking that the whole world must cater to their whims. Participating in a mission tour around the world with my college choir, I was shocked by the hostile attitudes toward the U.S. in many places. The contrast between our wealth and the poverty of the global community changed my life forever.

As a country we mistakenly think that God is on our side. How can he be when we are not in the center of his will to feed the hungry and clothe the naked and care for those that are homeless? How can we think we are his people when sexual immorality is so rampant in our society?

Revelation 2:27 quotes Psalm 2:9, part of a messianic passage proclaiming God's ultimate sovereignty over all the kings of the earth. We dare not think that our nation can have such sovereignty when we do not have the authority of moral uprightness. The authority that Jesus gives is that which he received from the Father, and he received it because he did the Father's will—constantly, obediently, faithfully. Only those who "do his will to the end" will have a similar authority. And they also receive the morning star.

Christ wants to be present in us and to impart his authority to us—our church communities, our country, our peoplehood. He calls us away from sexual immorality and sacrifices to other gods and empowers us instead to live in the center of his will.

Notes

1. Elizabeth O'Connor, "Learning from an Illness," *Cry Pain, Cry Hope: Thresholds to Purpose* (Waco, TX: Word Books, 1987), pp. 114–29, especially p. 114.
2. See Marva J. Dawn, "How Churches Can Deal with Teenage Immorality" in *Kardia,* the theological/ministerial journal of Western Evangelical Seminary in Portland, OR (1986). Teaching tapes on "Godly Sexuality" for teenagers and another one for parents are available from Christians Equipped for Ministry, Dottie Davis, tape editor, 15500 N.E. Caples Rd., Brush Prairie, WA 98606.

12

Sardis: A Call to Constant Renewal

Please refer often to Revelation 3:1–6 as you study this chapter.

At one point in a long medical struggle, a doctor tried a new medication to cut down swelling in my leg. It was supposed to stimulate nerves to signal blood vessels to constrict. However, it also made me so-o-o sleepy and not a little nauseous. I eagerly wanted to work on this book and prepare for speaking engagements, but I also desperately wanted to sleep. Which did I want more?

It was possible to shake off drowsiness and force myself to work because I always enjoy it in spite of illness, but it took a deliberate effort. I had to make a conscious choice and to back up that choice with straining exertion.

My difficulty in making choices parallels a problem in my spiritual life. In many aspects of it, I'd rather just sleep. It takes a deliberate effort for me to choose to engage in certain spiritual disciplines—to take time these nights for Advent devotions, to set aside time every week to participate in a Bible study group, to reserve special time for prayer. Periodically I need new motivation; regularly I need spiritual renewal. I suppose you do, too.

Consequently, the letter to the Christian community at Sardis is urgently valuable for us. The problem in that church has been repeated in the lives of God's people throughout their histories, for all kinds of forces draw us consistently away from a Christlike lifestyle.

Immediately the image of the Christlife is brought to our attention, for the beginning of this letter describes Christ as the one who holds the seven spirits and the seven stars. The combination of the two is significant.

Readers of this letter would no doubt instantly associate the seven spirits with the messianic prophecy of Isaiah 11:2, which declares that the Spirit of the LORD (the Almighty Yahweh, the covenant "I Am") would be on the shoot from the stump of Jesse. The first element of that sevenfold Spirit is that the branch from Jesse's roots would be filled with God's Spirit, perfectly attuned to doing the Father's will and living in complete reliance on him. Other aspects of the sevenfold spirit itemized in Isaiah 11 are the spirit of wisdom, understanding, counsel, strength, knowledge, and the fear of the Lord.

All of these aspects of the Christlife point to the indispensability of being aware of our weakness. We cannot be filled with the wisdom or understanding of God when we rely on the insufficiency of our own intellect and insights. We don't remain in the counsel of God when we think that the world's ways of doing things are adequate for the true tasks that need to be done. We consistently grasp for power when we deny our utter dependency on God. In our contemporary emphasis on information and computer data, we think we know everything that we need to know, but unless by God's grace we live in a personal and community relationship with God we cannot possibly know the meaning of his word, or of life, or of truth. Only God's grace can create a healthy balance of both knowing that we deserve God's wrath for our sinfulness and believing the assurance that we are loved anyway.

As stated earlier, the combination of the seven spirits and the seven stars in the description of Christ is significant. Not only does he call us personally to his own lifestyle, made possible by the indwelling of the whole Spirit of God in every aspect of our being, but also he calls the entire church. Revelation 1:20 told us that these seven stars are the angels of the seven churches—in other words, the representatives of representatives. The angels are the human leaders of the churches, or perhaps the spirit which characterizes them, and, as seen in the introduction to the letters in chapter 7 above, the churches were in prominent cities that seemed to serve as the focus for the whole region of Asia Minor. Consequently, when Christ says that he holds them in his hand, he reemphasizes this glorious truth of grace: that Christ always continues to hold his people in his care, no matter how desperately they need renewal.

He calls all of God's people everywhere to listen to this letter challenging the churches to new reliance on, and empowerment by, the Spirit.

Right away, the Christ who is so characterized berates the people of Sardis for their false front; he knows, though they appear to the rest of the world to be alive, that they are really spiritually dead. He does not criticize them for any particular sin, but simply for the fact that their deeds are not complete—and the only thing to do about that is to wake up!

The command is like an alarm clock that rings every few minutes: wake up! Strengthen the things that remain that were about to die! Remember what you have received and heard! Obey! Repent!

The ordering of those phrases is essential. We cannot strengthen what remains by ourselves. What we have received and heard—the Gospel!—revitalizes us. Our deeds, like those of the people of Sardis, are not complete in the sight of God, but God constantly calls us with the Gospel to new life, new hope, new response. This letter wakes us up to hear his call.

We have all missed opportunities, failed to use our spiritual gifts as fully as we could, or been spiritually dead in other ways. To my great regret, I did not use well a recent seven-month period of near blindness to learn lessons of listening to God. My constant "why" questions kept me from hearing God's answers to "what" he would strengthen instead.

Grace offers another path. When we would flounder in regrets or confusions, God wants to enable us instead to strengthen what remains. His grace empowers us for the disciplines that strengthen us; we respond to his immense love by spiritual exercise. For the people of Sardis the situation was critical—the things that remained were about to die. Our spiritual lives, too, shrink and get flabby without training. When we neglect the means God has provided for us to receive his grace—God's Word and prayer, the sacraments and forgiveness, his love incarnated in the Christian community—our spiritual lives get weak. Those gifts are given to strengthen what remains.

Two of my friends, out of their weakness, have taught me vital lessons about the importance and the gift of strengthening what remains. Linden, who is quadriplegic, illustrates by his physical discipline the importance of spiritual exercise. Though deprived of most upper-body functioning, he has chosen not to have an electric wheelchair so that he has to push himself wherever he goes. This strengthening of the one functioning muscle in his arms gives him amazing control of them so that he can cook, do photography, and even develop his own pictures. Similarly, when we receive God's grace through spiritual exercises of Word and worship, God empowers us to serve him in many ways.

Another friend, Connie, who is blind, demonstrated long ago the important lesson of rejoicing in what remains. She admitted to me that for a while she had been envious that I had not suffered diabetic complications affecting my eyes. (Since then I have lost half my vision and, for a while, most of it.) As she was praying about her attitude, she heard God's comfort to her so powerfully that it seemed almost audible. The voice assured her, "That's okay, Connie. For what I've called Marva to do, she needs her vision. For what I've called you to do, you don't necessarily need your eyes." (Connie is program director for Vision Northwest and helps 34 support groups and over 500 people in Oregon cope with the difficulties of living with visual impairment in a seeing world.)

Connie's words rang in my ears the next day when an orthopedic specialist informed me that I faced possible amputation of my foot. "It's okay," God says. "For what I've called you to do, you don't really need your feet." Connie's insight motivates me to write books as well as I can as long as eyes and brain and finger functions still remain. By myself I can't accept my crippled leg and diminished eyesight, but coping with the loss is made easier by the challenge to focus instead on God's gifts to strengthen what still remains.

The Christians at Sardis are commanded to remember—a common scriptural theme—what they have received and heard. Constantly God urges us to remember what he has taught, how he has intervened in history, what we have learned from the traditions of faith. The Gospel in our memories, then, leads to these results: obedience and repentance. As we hear again God's exhortations, we want to respond with eager acceptance of his commands and desires and will, and we are sorry for the many times we have failed to respond positively. Our repentance (the Greek *metanoia*) is a genuine turning around of both thought and behavior.

SARDIS: A CALL TO CONSTANT RENEWAL

All the warnings of the letter to Sardis summarize excellently the elements needed for true renewal. Growing spirituality requires a steady repetition of the truths of faith, which will lead to repentance for our failures, a turning around of mind and deed, a desire to strengthen what remains, and an eagerness to obey in the future. Moreover, we often need a summons to new spiritual alertness.

Christ says there are a few in the church at Sardis who have not soiled their clothes. In context with all the rest of the Scriptures, this certainly cannot mean that these people do not need renewal or that they are without sin. Rather, their lives are already constantly being renewed. Since only Christ's grace makes us worthy to walk with him, they are undoubtedly folk who are constantly aware of their need for his guidance and, therefore, are people who have not soiled their clothes by wandering far away from his truth or by becoming proud of their own purity.

They are given as examples. If any others in the church can overcome (which means in this context to repent and be renewed), they, too, can become like these models. All who overcome will know the same purity. They are promised that they will all be dressed in white. Their renewal in faith will keep their names in the book of life, and they will, therefore, be acknowledged by Christ in heaven.

We in the 20th century also have some models, people who are constantly seeking renewal in their faith and, as a result, live with faithfulness and purity. Those who recognize their own weakness and trust God's empowerment provide excellent models. I think, for example, of Joni Eareckson Tada, whose faith has radiated from her wheelchair and touched thousands of lives. This past weekend she and I were on the same airplane, so I could observe the great love of God with which she greeted all whom she encountered. Another who trusted God to strengthen what remained was Toni Carson, who did not let her painful cancer prevent her from organizing prayer groups for her children's schools. Similarly, Audrey Kershner, a senior citizen I met through my childhood paper route, continued to pray for me and to inspire me throughout her beautifully Christlike life. Christians in Mexico taught me out of their poverty what it means to share.

Moreover, there are many living saints now in the congregation to which I belong whose lives call me to renewal. A motorcyclist drove me to the bus last week and told me wonderful stories of God at work through him in his travels; an elderly couple drove far out of their way to take me to worship when I was still single and a stranger in the congregation; in response to our pastor's prayer in worship for my physical needs, the woman in charge of receptions sent a lovely note assuring me of her help with our wedding; another retired member answered my call for transportation in an emergency.

Certainly in your Christian community you also could name some models who can teach the rest of us more of what the faith life means. Their spiritual example invites us to wake up, to remember, to repent, to obey afresh, to strengthen what remains so that we can serve God to the best of our ability for the rest of our days.

13

Philadelphia: An Open Door

Please refer often to Revelation 3: 7–13 as you study this chapter.

How inspiring that God is able to use us powerfully when we are weak! My friend Toni, who battled breast cancer that metastasized to the lungs and brain, strengthened the faith of many people with her incredible tenacity of trust in God's wisdom and care. She experienced God's healing grace in a remarkable extension of life, but she also courageously faced the ravages of her illness with the true hope that only weakness can bring.

What a glorious promise we receive when Christ declares in the letter to the saints at Philadelphia that the ones with little strength will become pillars. They have kept Christ's word and have not denied his name. They have endured patiently and so will be spared the hour of trial that will test the whole world.

As usual, the description of Christ is singularly appropriate. The letter begins with a picture of him as the holy and true one, the one who holds the key of David, the one whose opening and shutting no one can oppose. It is amazing that in his holiness he can look at our weakness and commend it. How different the values of Christ are from those of the world, which praises the ones who are beautiful, successful, rich, ambitious, skillful, powerful. We humans praise such things because we are not holy, and in our lack of perfection we fumble for the "best," which seems to be epitomized by those who seem to have it all.

In contrast, the holy/set apart One sets apart those who know they are not at the top of the ladder. He who is true praises those who speak the truth about their inadequacies and do not claim any false superiorities.

He holds the power to open and close all that pertains to the true Israel, for he holds the key of David. Therefore, he can open a door before those who are humble. He knows them truly—that they are not falsely pretending to be greater than they are—and so he gives them unrestricted entrance. The sky isn't even the limit to what they can do in his name.

Christ gives those with little strength an open door. Sadly, if we get too caught up in the world's success syndrome, we might try to close it. Sometimes in our churches we shut out the weak and prevent them from offering their gifts to the community. Actually, we cannot ultimately shut the door, for no one can shut what Christ has opened. The weak who depend on him will serve him and become what he has in store for them with or without our approval and care, but in the process we lose the gifts they could bring to the Body.

Perhaps we are numbered among those who are of "the synagogue of Satan." In the time when The Revelation was written, that phrase may have designated the group that history calls the Judaizers—those who tried to force Jewish practices on Gentile believers. In so doing, they negated the Gospel of freedom and grace in Christ. Similarly, in the 20th century, many who claim to participate in Christianity negate its tenets. Certainly anytime we block the purposes of God by our own petty prejudices we are serving the synagogue of Satan rather than the temple of God. When we make demands, we negate the grace that sets us all free.

This letter challenges each of us to look at our attitudes and actions toward the weak. Christ says that he will make all those who lie to come and fall down at the feet of the weak and acknowledge that he has loved them. In modern society we often lie about God's love for the weak by our own refusal truly to welcome them into our fellowships. Maybe we lie about God's love for them by not helping to care for their physical needs. Sometimes our lies are more subtle—inward attitudes that we don't reveal, hidden animosities that we hide, repressed impatience that we don't vent.

Three times this section uses the word *Behold!* to call our attention to what we usually fail to notice. God shows very clearly that those who have little strength—in whatever form that might take in history—are the special objects of his concern. The mentally deficient are often very sure about his love and dearly capable of loving others. Those whose handicaps make them utterly reliant on God's strength are often profoundly taught by their situation to forego the world's methods of power. If we are caught up in our own capabilities, we won't notice such things now, but we will someday.

Moreover, Christ declares that he is coming soon. How can we reconcile this promise of quick fulfillment with its delay of almost 2,000 years?

The fact is, Christ *is* coming soon, regardless of how that works out in the history of the earth. It requires weakness for us to recognize that such a length of time does not falsify the promise.

When I began to use insulin at the age of 16 because measles had killed my pancreas, my life span as a brittle diabetic was forecast to be limited. Then in my 40th year my doctor suggested gently that this is probably my last decade. These forecasts have been very valuable—not to scare me, but instead to make me know a healthy sense of urgency that I wish everybody had. Most of my life has been undergirded with a deep, abiding recognition that I must use time well. (That doesn't mean not to have fun, because using time well also means keeping the Sabbath and enjoying God's design for rest.[1])

For me there has always been a sense that Christ is coming soon in my life. That actually frees me to care more about people, to wonder about their salvation, to choose more deliberately what I do with my time.

Christ commands those with little strength in Philadelphia to hold fast to what they have so that no one will take their crown. Perhaps they have been persecuted for so long that they wonder if they can hold out any longer. God's gift of the crown of life enables them to continue persevering. Even so, the anticipation of Christ's coming soon, the experience of his gracious coming now into our lives, and the process of holding fast to faith meanwhile enable us to enjoy that crown to some extent even now. We have already been crowned with the Joy promised in the messianic age (Is. 35:10), which makes us look forward all the more to the perfection of Joy we will experience someday when all the present tears and pain, the sorrow and sighing, will flee away.

We must be very careful when we discuss the tribulation from which the Philadelphians will be spared. It grieves me that Revelation 3:10 is often taken out of context, improperly joined together with Luke 17:34–36 and 1 Thessalonians 4:17 (which speak of entirely different things in their original contexts), and made into "the rapture." This procedure constructs a major doctrine on the basis of a misreading of the texts.

Instead, a major rule for reading Scripture accurately is that each verse must be read in its own context. In the contexts of the words of Christ in Luke 17, the verses about "one taken and the other left" mean that Christ will come suddenly and that we won't know who is part of his kingdom. Chapter 4 of Thessalonians was originally intended to comfort people who had already lost loved ones before the expected return of Christ. The apostle Paul offers this hope to them: they will all be together when Christ comes. He uses the image of Christ gathering everyone in the clouds (the symbol throughout the Bible of God's presence) to assure his mourning readers that in the future they will be together both with God and with those who had already died. These verses in Revelation 3 about being spared the tribulation cannot be disassociated from the words to the people in Smyrna that they would suffer in the coming peril. Not all Christians will be spared the suffering.

Such differing contexts in Luke, Thessalonians, and Revelation prohibit an indiscriminate conjoining of isolated texts. Each passage must first be studied for its intended meaning for the original readers, out of which will come its lessons for application to the present times.

Furthermore, some groups who read these verses out of their historical and literary context also spend much of their time debating the "when" of the rapture, even though Jesus specifically told his followers in several places (such as Luke 17:23 and 21:8) that they should not chase after the people who claim to know about the time of the end. Since we do not know how the world will end, how Christ will come or when, how we will be taken from this world to be with him, and so forth, we would do much better not to speculate about such things and instead to concentrate on these messages that Christ gave us for the meanwhile: repent, watch, tell others, do justice and mercy, walk humbly with God. Perhaps one aspect of weakness I have not stressed enough yet is the weakness of not knowing, of accepting that certain dimensions of God's kingdom are beyond our ken.

What Jesus does promise to the Philadelphians is delightful. Not only will they not ever have to leave the temple of God, but they will be pillars. Those whom the world thought were weak will be revealed as those with the strength to hold up the place where God dwells. The kingdom of God is carried not by strength according to the world's idea, but by the weakness that lets God's grace shine through. Those who suffer or grow faint already wear the crowns that cannot be taken. Their mettle will someday be proved, to the astonishment of those who served Satan's purposes by buying into the world's stratagems for power. Those who scorned the weak will discover that faithful people with little strength are the beloved of God.

The other promises of the letter to Philadelphia are equally encouraging. The ones overcoming by holding on in their weakness and consequent humility will be inscribed with several names. Remember that the idea of "name" in the Scriptures always refers to the character of the one named. That is why, for example, we can know that our prayers will be answered when we pray in the name of Christ, for, holding his character in our consciousness, we would only pray for what accords with God's will.

Thus, to receive God's name means that someday those who lack strength will become totally fashioned after the likeness of God. Furthermore, they will receive the name of the city of God, the New Jerusalem, which will be described later in The Revelation. Then in John's vision we shall observe all the glory and splendor and purity that will be manifested at the end of time through those who depended on God. Finally, Christ promises that he will even write on them *his* new name. Throughout the Scriptures we read that at the end of time, having finished all the work that the Father gave him to do, Christ will be magnified above all. In that supreme exaltation, he will share his character with those who trusted him in spite of their weakness. The Scriptures never give such a promise to those who trust their own capabilities. Only by profound humility does one truly enter into the grace of Christ, which makes possible participation in his greatest glory.

Of all the letters to the churches in Revelation 2 and 3, this one most thoroughly underscores my plea to value our own weakness and to encourage others with little strength in our Christian communities. Only as we all become totally dependent on God and his grace will we find ourselves part of this great company that will receive the very name of God at the end of time.

Notes

1. See Marva J. Dawn, *Keeping the Sabbath Wholly: Ceasing, Resting, Embracing, Feasting* (Grand Rapids, MI: Wm. B. Eerdmans Publishing Co., 1989).

14

Laodicea: Whatever Our Limitations, We Don't Have to Be Tepid

Please refer often to Revelation 3:14–22 as you study this chapter.

The waiter looked at me in surprise. I had asked him to take the teapot back to the kitchen and bring me one with *boiling* water. I did not mean to be obnoxious, but tea bags just cannot pour out their flavor unless the water is scalding. What a treasure—a steaming pot of herbal tea!

The letter to the Laodiceans in Revelation 3 is often misunderstood because we don't properly interpret the image of water that is hot, cold, or lukewarm. Many people who talk about this text use the cold side of the dichotomy to emphasize that often those who are the most violently opposed to the kingdom of God are the closest to entering it. Certainly this is an observable phenomenon: atheists or agnostics sometimes move suddenly from a vicious opposition to the Gospel to a surprising and very warm acceptance of it. Indeed, they do rapidly change from being very cold to being very hot.

However, it could hardly be the case that the Lord of the church is here advocating such coldness nor that he would think it desirable for persons to be violently opposed to the Gospel—even though it might suddenly become real to them. Though they might become very warm in their appreciation of his message after the initial rejection, we can hardly imagine him saying, "I *wish* that you were cold, that you would spurn my truth."

Rather, we must understand that the letter to the church at Laodicea fits in very well with the actual geographical circumstances of that city. Its message poignantly rebukes the Christians there because its water image is true to their experience and thereby underscores the point more forcibly.[1]

Laodicea was an extremely difficult city to defend because it lacked its own water supply. Aqueducts brought drinking water from the springs near Denizli, six miles to the south. Moreover, Colossae, the site 10 miles away of a sister church to the one in Laodicea, was known for its cold, pure waters. By the time water got to Laodicea from the cold springs, however, it was tepid—not very refreshing.

On the other hand, six miles to the north of Laodicea were the hot mineral springs of Hierapolis. However, by the time the healing and restorative waters flowed across a wide plateau and over a broad escarpment opposite Laodicea, they were naturally lukewarm—not soothing.

Thus, the Holy Spirit's message to the church at Laodicea is very clear: don't be like your water—lukewarm from the journey, neither invigorating nor healing, but merely to be spewed out (the Spanish says "vomitar"). The message projects a clarion call to decisive commitment, as well as the recognition that our commitment functions in different ways according to the needs. At certain times our dedication will be manifested in soothing warmth—comforting words, gentle caressing of weary spiritual muscles. Sometimes we serve as a Jacuzzi in our ministry to others. On the other hand, at times we must serve as an ice water drink, to refresh, motivate, resuscitate. We serve as prophets, stirring up people and alerting them to the dangers of sloth or greed.

Just as first-century people chose the waters of Hieropolis or Colossae according to their health concern, so in the 20th century we must become more discerning and learn whether to minister to others with a cold plunge or a hot sauna. Paul instructs the church at Thessalonica to "admonish the unruly, encourage the fainthearted, help the weak, and be patient with all" (1 Thess. 5:14). Our care for one another must match the need.

In that discernment, however, we must not forget our theology of weakness. Our ability to minister as either warm or cold springs does not come from our own efforts to produce a certain degree of water. The middle portion of the letter to Laodicea (Rev. 3:16–18) warns us against such presumption.

LAODICEA: WE DON'T HAVE TO BE TEPID

The problem with the folks in Laodicea was that they had too many things going for them. Because the city was so prosperous, they weren't aware of their desperate need for grace. They did not know the weakness and dependence that are essential for true ministry in Christ. First-century Laodicea was famous for many things, and the members of the church there probably participated in the well-being of the city. In contrast to the church at Smyrna, this congregation was probably more comfortably self-sufficient.

The city of Laodicea was renowned for its financial institutions. Supposedly, even the philosopher Cicero banked his money there. Consequently, it makes sense that the message of the Spirit should remind the believers there not to trust in human gold. Instead, the members of the Laodicean community are to buy from the Lord of the church his gold, which has truly been purified by means of fire. Then they will have genuine riches.

Though financial resources are undoubtedly helpful, we must always remember that human wealth does not in and of itself accomplish God's purposes. This message is urgently needed in our times, when so many of the churches of the U.S. seem to think that prosperity is essential to serve God.

There are enough harangues against ostentatious riches in the church to make it unnecessary for me to add another. Moreover, we all have a basic concern for the poor, which causes us to want to keep in balance our own use of wealth. However, reliance on human gold often creeps in when we are unaware.

Jacques Ellul's insightful book *Money and Power*[2] points out the subtle ways in which the false god Mammon so easily deceives us and commands our allegiance. We worry about not having enough money; we hoard it; we use it carefully and in our "responsible stewardship" lose the generosity of grace; or we become too proud of our refusal to accumulate it.

We need immense vigilance to fight the enculturation to which we are so susceptible. Once we start to let thoughts of human wealth control us, the god Mammon takes over more and more.

A radical example (by "radical" I mean "getting to the root of the issue") might help to make my point. When I first began writing, I decided that all royalty monies would be given to charitable organizations—not only to free me from writing to please the market, but also because I didn't earn enough as a freelancer to be able to give away very much. Book royalties provide the means to share with the poor, though at some point my declining health might necessitate using the income to support Christians Equipped for Ministry (the corporation under which I freelance) so that I can keep writing.

Once when a royalty check arrived (in the days before I had arranged with publishers to send royalties directly to specific ministries), I was tempted to question my previous decision about such monies. I was in graduate school in the Midwest and yearned to visit my friends on the West Coast. Perhaps I could keep for myself just enough to buy one plane ticket.

However, it became apparent immediately how hard it would be for me to draw the line! If I kept some for myself to buy a plane ticket to the West, then why not more? In fact, why not keep all of it, and then I could afford several trips over the next years to visit my friends? When I realized what was happening, I knew it had to be all or nothing. Keeping any of the money for this one trip would too easily lead to hoarding it all for myself.

A few days later a friend suggested that I should instead just keep out enough money for a few long distance phone calls. It certainly wouldn't be selfish to give myself a few pleasures, I rationalized—the delight of talking with distant friends would certainly be a boost to my studies. And then, of course, a little could be set aside for celebrations—just enough to go out for ice cream (my chief vice) or to enjoy a concert with friends.

Once again, the amount I would "need" began to multiply. How easily my selfishness spread, and I got more and more covetous of things (ice cream cones) and experiences (talking with or visiting friends far away) until once again all of the money was in my possession.

The use of one small royalty check might seem a petty issue, but it presented to me a major ethical decision. The situation forced me to confront my own tendency to multiply my "needs," in contrast to an earlier careful determination to follow Jesus' command to share wealth so that others less fortunate than myself might also have opportunities for well-being and education.

My graduate assistantships were certainly adequate for all my needs, and there was plenty left over for celebrations if I lived carefully. Only selfish greed prompted the sudden yearning to keep royalty money for myself. The whole issue forced me to face our human craving to accumulate and to realize how easily we are misled from our desire to live as Christ would have us live in simple, more extensive sharing with others.

So easily our churches and our personal Christian lives become enculturated! We think we *need* all the things that make for a pleasant life. As our income increases, our needs and desires grow to match it. Unless we choose deliberately to live more simply and to care more intentionally for others, we can easily spend all that we have.

Tragically, the First World has been doing that for centuries. The rich have become richer and the poor have become poorer, because we have not taken the first steps to follow Jesus in how we use our money.

The idea is intriguing—compelling! What would happen if we took seriously Christ's command to sell what we have and give to the poor, if we cut short our growing propensity to accumulate and said, "Thus far will my budget go and no farther" (with apologies to the book of Job for the paraphrase)?

The other two images in the letter to the Laodiceans make the same point. The city was well-known for its medical facilities and, especially, for a special salve prepared there for the treatment of eye problems. Also, Laodicea produced illustrious garments made out of a beautiful black wool taken from sheep who grazed in the area. Consequently, the Spirit cautions the church that they should recognize their need to be clothed in white garments (always the symbol of restoration and purity in the Scriptures) and to be treated with an eye salve that would enable them to see spiritually. All dependence on human resources to see, to be clothed, or to possess wealth should be recognized for what it truly is: a dependence on that which could not meet their deepest needs, with the result that they were "afflicted, miserable, begging poor, blind and naked." Human resources are bound to fail.

Christians are called to a different response. Christ, the "faithful and true witness" (3:14), reminds us that he reproves and disciplines us out of his love for us (3:19). Therefore, we are challenged to respond with zeal and repentance. Christ himself is at the door, and he is knocking. If anyone hears his voice and opens the door, he will enter into that person and will eat with her and she with him.

This is plain and simple: Jesus calls us to repentance. We must begin by recognizing that we have turned to false values and gods when we have mistaken human goods for the things of God, and we must recognize that we desperately need the Lord's discipline and instruction.

This text also gives great comfort for many reasons. First of all, the ones whom the Lord reproves are the ones he loves. The original Greek word for "reprove" means "to bring to light" in the sense of exposing or correcting, but because that reproof comes from love it is not an exposure that destroys us.

In contrast, the word for "to discipline" means "to educate, to bring up with training." That idea, too, offers comfort. My parents trained me in all sorts of things—not only in the basics of my Christian faith, but also in the skills of pitching and hitting baseballs, in the arts of cooking and cleaning, in appreciation of good music. Out of their love, my parents brought me up to know how to do many things—not only for useful purposes, but also for enjoyment.

In the same way, the Lord instructs us not only in the things that we might do in his service, but also in the things that give our lives value and purpose and meaning. Therefore, knowing that his reproof and discipline are designed to develop our Christian character, we respond zealously and repent for whatever keeps us from loving him in all aspects of our life. We know that we need to change our mind about many things in order to have the mind of Christ.

Revelation 3:20 is misused in Christian circles if, in evangelism programs, it is used to describe the relationship of Jesus to people who do not yet believe in him. I have heard many Christians tell nonbelievers, "If you just recognize that Jesus is standing at the door of your heart and knocking to get in, if you will just open the door, then he will come in, and he will remain with you and have fellowship with you." To use this verse in such a way is to read the passage improperly and to make ourselves (because *we* open the door) the agents of God's redeeming grace.

The first major rule for using the Scriptures is to keep them appropriately in their context. This verse is not addressing non-Christians, who need to repent and to come to faith. Instead, it refers to Christians who have failed to trust God for their wealth and health and covering. Believers are to repent and recognize that Christ is at the door in his desire to come into their lives more deeply. We shut him out when we succumb to the temptation to trust money and possessions and human remedies for our happiness. In our failure to repent we miss his purposes for our lives. If we become zealous to choose God's ways more intentionally, then we will experience the presence of Christ more deeply. The promise of eating with him implies the kind of fellowship that Christians can enjoy in God's company.

To experience Christ's presence in this way was the outcome of the situation described earlier in which I was tempted to hoard royalty money for myself. After the money was safely sent away and no longer a temptation, many subsequent events showed me how richly God continues to provide for all my needs and even my enjoyments without my having to be selfish. The situation also made very clear how much I need to repent for my false trust in human gods.

Awareness of our failures and the limits of our human weaknesses and appreciation for the riches of God's resources cause us to be more zealous to repent and to find his grace sufficient for all our needs. Truly he will give us gold refined in the fire, garments that are white and pure, eye salve that will enable us to see spiritually, and his very own presence to sustain us. Then we can live out the commitment to which the first part of this passage calls us: to be not as the lukewarm water, which has traveled a great distance over plateaus or through aqueducts, but as the healing hot springs or the invigorating cold springs themselves—comforting or stimulating one another as we seek to serve the Lord with full commitment.

Notes

1. This chapter's information about the city of Laodicea—its waters, banks, medical school, and sheep for black wool—was taken from Robert H. Mounce's commentary on *The Book of Revelation, The New International Commentary on the New Testament,* F. F. Bruce, gen. ed. (Grand Rapids, MI: Wm. B. Eerdmans Publishing Co., 1977), pp. 122–30.

2. Jacques Ellul, *Money and Power,* LaVonne Neff, trans. (Downers Grove, IL: Inter-Varsity Press, 1964).

15

The First Reason
for Praise: The Gift of Life

Please refer often to Revelation 4:1–11 as you study this chapter.

Tim's dialysis room before his marriage was gaily decorated with bright red and blue festoons, ropes of brilliant plastic looping from one corner to the other. Several other cords hung like crepe-paper garlands across each other and down the walls so that the room hardly seemed like a place for serious medical treatment. It couldn't be austere with those colorful festival ribbons.

The impression they made on Tim's visitors, however, changed drastically when they learned that those celebrative festoons were made of the ends of the artificial kidneys used on his dialysis machine. Each one of the red and blue inch-long pieces of plastic represented more than eight hours on the machine, so those long, draping cords pictured years of added life, the gift of modern technology, the grace of a machine to cleanse Tim's blood and stave off death.

Each year I celebrate the anniversary of his first dialysis run (the date is written in my birthday book) because those treatments make possible the gift of his friendship. I met Tim a few years after his kidneys failed, so I was always conscious when I visited that room that the treasures of his love and all the lessons I have learned from him are especially gracious presents.

Similarly, in various periods when my insulin balance has been crazy, when I have felt the fragility of life gone totally out of control, I have remembered afresh the precious gift of a God-designed human body with all its profound interrelations. How amazingly all the parts of our systems continue to function and support each other with incredible regularity and precision—just the right amount of hormones, the proper beating of heart and pulsing of lungs and blood, the right exchanges of carbon dioxide and oxygen, the appropriate rate of metabolism. How can anyone look seriously at the gift of life and not acknowledge a Creator?

How wonder-full that a normal person's pancreas automatically introduces into the lifeblood exactly the amount of insulin needed to keep blood glucose levels precisely where they should be. Diabetics constantly have to judge how much insulin to inject. My extreme brittleness causes severe insulin reactions if I work too hard or don't eat enough. On the other hand, the difficulties of controlling glucose levels lead to the kinds of complications I am experiencing after 29 years on insulin—loss of feeling and crippling in the feet and hands, hemorrhaging in the eyes, malfunctioning of the intestines, inability to heal after injuries, susceptibility to gangrene, deficient metabolism and resultant slowness and pain. How I long for a body that functions properly so that I wouldn't have to be adjusting all the time to new troubles!

However, I must honestly say that I am grateful for these snags because they remind me that life is a treasure to be stewarded and celebrated. I certainly need their reminder not to take all God's stupendous gifts for granted.

Revelation 4 points to the gift of life as one reason for praise. The progression leading to that conclusion, however, also suggests an important process for us to undergo so that we will value praise more deeply and enter into it with greater Joy.

The story begins (4:1, "after this," after the dictating of the seven letters) with the seer John being invited into a new vision of that which lies on the other side of the door of heaven, where he will be able to see the things that must necessarily happen "after this." There is no direct antecedent to this second use of the phrase "after this." Since the subsequent vision takes the seer to the heavens, we might assume that "this" refers to the time of trials, since the book is specifically addressed, as we have seen, to those who are suffering the tribulation of governmental persecution and societal alienation. After the time of testing, after the pain of this world, then all will be restored as we go through the door into the Joy of a perfect life in relationship with God.

Next the seer reports that, being immediately ushered in spirit into the heavens, he became aware of the throne of God. How vital it is for us to catch visions of that throne to restore our perspectives in life on this side of the door!

We cannot properly learn to praise unless we begin at the throne, for praise is the recognition that God is there, that he is the ruler of our lives and all that is, that he is worthy of our adoration. In other words, praise prevents us from focusing on ourselves. It is wonderfully theocentric.

John's description of the throne and its occupant is magnificent—and terribly inadequate. No matter how splendiferously we might picture it, we could never capture the overwhelming magnificence of God's throne and the glory of his presence in human, finite words—that's why I sometimes have to make them up! However, the richness of the seer's inspired description here begins to capture for us (until we actually experience it in glory) the transcendence that we must understand to view the throne now with praise.

That the seer is using the best possible, but yet inadequate, words to describe his vision is indicated by his reference to the radiance as that of a rainbow like an emerald. He probably didn't mean that the rainbow had only one color (green) or that it was stony, for he also talks about the one on the throne in terms of the stones jasper and sardius. These gems were the best available images in the first century to describe tremendous beauty and value.

The picture of a rainbow's radiance around the LORD comes from Ezekiel 1:28 and reminds us of the entire context of the description there and its significance for the Jews in the Babylonian captivity, but the seer has added the idea of the emerald. Surely he was overwhelmed by the lushness of the vision he had been privileged to see on the other side of the door.

Next he talks about the population of that heavenly scene—24 elders dressed in white garments and golden wreaths. White garments are used throughout The Revelation to indicate perfection and purity (see 3:5, 18; 6:11; 7:9, 13; 19:14), and the golden wreaths remind us of royal splendor and victory. The idea of the elders being with the ruler gloriously comes from Isaiah 24:23, but their number is not given in that Hebrew text. The number 12 is used frequently in The Revelation, especially in chapter 7, where it is multiplied by itself and used in connection with the names of Jacob's sons. The number 12 always represents the people of God. Even as there were 12 tribes of Israel and Jesus had most likely chosen 12 apostles to represent the continuation of the people of God, now the doubling of the number seems to indicate that these elders represent all of God's people, from both the first covenant (Israel) and the second (the church).

The seer interrupts his description of the occupants of the throne room to comment again on its radiance and majesty, and that element of this chapter's style hints at the awe with which it was written. The literary montage reminds me of a child, full of good things to tell his mother, running into the house and crying out, "And then I saw this . . . and look at that . . . and oh, yes, they were so big . . . but oh, that was so wonderful!" The seer can hardly keep pace with his impressions as he jumps from the magnificence of the stones, to the rainbow radiance, to the golden-wreathed elders, to the lightnings and thunders, to the strange-looking creatures. The vision stuns with spiraling collages of splendor that human words can hardly begin to describe.

A note must be inserted here about the nature of the biblical writings. More and more contemporary theology accentuates the humanity of the Scriptures, which results in great doubt about the concept of inspiration. The two components—human and divine—must be kept in dialectical tension. Certainly the Holy Spirit thoroughly inspired the apostles and prophets as they wrote, and the resultant books of the Bible are definitely God's Word to his people and authoritative for their lives. On the other hand, the writers were not mechanical robots as they recorded the Spirit's message. Each writer's personality is evident; his style is unique. They wrote under the limitation of human words and invite us into their wonder at the infinity of God's majesty and grace. We jump into the awe and are astonished and speechless; we know the limits of human words to articulate our Joy and terror and delight.

The heavenly throne room is like the first meeting of Dorothy with the Wizard of Oz, when she sees the lightning and hears the voices and thunders, but here there is no deceptive man behind the curtain pulling the levers. Instead there are seven lamps blazing, representing the seven spirits of God (perhaps a reference to Is. 11:1). With its lightning and peals of thunder, the scene reminds us of the terrifying appearance of God on Mount Sinai (see Ex. 19:18), so it carries implications of his covenant relationship with his people.

Finally, before the throne there is a sea of glass, which looks like rock crystal—an image from Ezekiel 1:22. That reference from the First Testament gives us a hint at its reason, for the description of the expanse can be translated as "sparkling like ice." I remember the bright vision on a sunny day of the Mendenhall glacier in Juneau, Alaska, with all its glintings and gleamings of sparkling ice. Refracting and dancing all around my head, the myriad beams of light sent shafts of blazing glory through my whole body and filled me with wonder. Imagine the reflection of the heavenly throne's brilliance from such an expanse of icy glass!

Next, the seer describes the four living creatures (again in images taken from Ezek. 1) with faces like those of a lion, an ox, a man, and an eagle. This bizarre picture of four-faced creatures from Ezekiel is then combined with the drama of Isaiah 6, where the seraphim (literally, fiery beings) have six wings, are full of eyes, and sing throughout the day and night in marvelous antiphony these words of praise: "Holy, holy, holy, LORD God, the Almighty." However, instead of declaring next that the whole earth is full of his glory, as the song does in Isaiah, the song in The Revelation continues with a reminder that the Lord is the one who was and the one who is and the one who is to come—also an image from Isaiah, but from other sections of the prophecy. This song, therefore, reminds us again of the uniquely unchanging nature of the God whom we are worshiping. The fact that the four living creatures do not cease to sing the hymn suggests that we can't ever sufficiently praise God for who he is, nor can we ever comprehend the meaning of his infinity.

As the drama in Isaiah 6 continues, the prophet cannot cope with his experience of seeing the holy God. He responds, "Woe is me, for I am *annihilated* [Luther's emphasis], for I have seen the LORD." That is not the creatures' response here in Revelation 4, for they don't have such a sense of shame and trepidation. Rather, the text goes on to say that they give the one on the throne all the glory and honor and thanks. For our purposes now, we observe how much these terms put into the center the one sitting on the throne. He is celebrated as living into the aeons of the aeons and thereby finally receiving all the glory and honor and thanks that are due him.

At this point all the elders are overwhelmed; they fall on their faces before the one on the throne and offer him their reverence. They throw their wreaths before the throne because they know that truly he is the victor who deserves their crowns. Once again the text reminds us that this one on the throne lives forever and ever—his eternity has been summarized three times already in as many verses.

This piling up of images is intended to create an atmosphere of great awesomeness, to surround us with a profound sense of wonder at the privilege of our relationship with such a one, at the splendor of knowing him who has no time, even though we are limited by it now. We rejoice to be swept up into the song that fills the heavens and closes the scene in its exultation of his worthiness.

All these images, stirring in us a heightened sense of mystery and magnificence, now culminate in the declaration of why God is worthy of such praise. Surely all the accoutrements of the scene have prepared us for this splendor, but now the declaration is explicit. God is indeed worthy of our adoration because by his will all things were created. The idea of his creation here at the end of the Bible reminds us of the pictures of his work of ordering at the beginning. This God who could bring existence out of the chaotic mass without form and full of nothingness (or vanity) is certainly worthy of our praising recognition of his power. Furthermore, the song declares that having once given order and form he does not leave the creation to its own devices, but remains the means by which that creation has its being. By his will he sustains all life; by his grace he allows it to continue. The combination of a Greek aorist tense (once for all) declaration of creation with an imperfect tense (continuing) state of being reminds us that everything, from beginning to end and everywhere in between, is totally under his perfect control.

Just as Tim's festoons of kidney valves gloriously display the wonder of a precious life kept alive by modern technology (which is God's servant), so we each need this picture of the one on the throne, by whose will we are sustained, in order to put the gift of life into its proper perspective. One of the reasons I value the feeble and the infirm and the elderly in my life is that they continually remind me of the fragility of our existence. Let none of us take this gift of life for granted.

The one who sits on the throne, the holy one who was and is and always shall be, the one whose magnificent environment heightens his claim on our adoration, has by his most gracious will designed and sustained all creation. That is the first reason why we are invited by the seer to learn better to praise God. Our next chapter will give us an even more important reason.

16

The Second Reason for Praise: The Lamb Who Saves by Suffering

Please refer often to Revelation 5:1–14 as you study this chapter.

The mystery baffled everyone. Only the redoubtable Sherlock Holmes could solve it, and then only with intensive efforts and great care. He alone could find the murderer of the heiress.

The fifth chapter of The Revelation poses a more difficult case. Near the magnificent throne described in the previous chapter is a book sealed with the perfect number (seven) of seals. The book has been written on both inside and out, so that it is full of important messages, but no one is able to unlock its mysteries. Such a book was previously imaged in Ezekiel 2:9–10, where the prophet was given a scroll written on both inside and out with words of lamentation, mourning, and woe, and in Isaiah 29:11–12, where that prophet speaks of a sealed scroll that no one is able to read. The picture here in The Revelation might also hint at the end of the book of Daniel (12:4), where the prophet is told to seal up the words of prophecy because they concerned the distant future, which should not yet be known, and at Psalm 139:16, which praises God for the fact that all the days of the poet's life had been ordained before he was born and were written in the Lord's book.

Now in the seer's vision the voice of a "strong angel" calls out for someone to open the scroll, but even the angel is not able to break the seals. In all of heaven, all the earth, and all the underworld there is no Sherlock Holmes able to unlock the mystery.

Note especially the seer's reaction to this state of affairs: he is absolutely devastated by it. What a great tragedy that no one is able to unlock the secrets of the great scroll! The original Greek says that the seer was crying vehemently because there was no one worthy. Remember that even the strength of the mighty angel who had called out was not sufficient. Power cannot unlock the secrets of the mysteries of God; the task requires worthiness.

One of the 24 elders offers a comforting word: Indeed, there is one great enough to open the scroll, and that individual is described in terms of power and strength. He is named the victor (obviously one with power great enough to overcome all opposition) and the lion of the tribe of Judah. The lion is always associated with devastation of its prey and here fulfills Jacob's deathbed prediction (see Gen. 49:8–9) that Judah will have his hand on the neck of his enemies because he is a lion's cub and, like a lion, crouches and lies down. Finally, the one who is able to open the scroll and its seals is called the Root of David, which brings to mind all the promises that David's house would always rule over the nation of Israel, for his reign was her epitome of victory and military strength.

All these titles and their contexts in the First Testament prepare us for an image of great strength, daring, and devastation of the enemy. We are not at all ready for the appearance of this one Who is called worthy, for he comes as a lamb, and not only as such a gentle creature, but also as a lamb that has been slain.

Furthermore, the original Greek verb tense underscores the thoroughness of that slaying; because the Lamb was once slain, the benefits of that slaying remain for us. Thus, the Lamb's worthiness lies in what his suffering conveys.

Yet this Lamb, standing as one having been slaughtered, has seven horns (the perfect number of symbols of power) and seven eyes (having perfect insight and understanding), which are the seven spirits of God (probably a reference to the prophecy in Is. 11:1 that the Lord's shoot from Jesse's stump—again a messianic expectation—will be endowed with the sevenfold spirit of God). In this endowment of the spirit, he has the power to reach out to all the earth. This is the one who is able to take the scroll.

Because of the glaring contrast between the names of victor, lion, and Root of Jesse, and their actual fulfillment in the Lamb who was slain, we are forced to recognize this major theme of the New Testament in its entirety and particularly in The Revelation: the victory comes through sacrifice.

This theme is critically important in the 20th century, which emphasizes victory through domination. We have certainly seen the demonic effects of demagogical power in the rise of Nazi tyranny and of despotic communism. Surely our society ought to be more afraid of power than it is. However, it seems that all who aspire to power think that it will not corrupt them, that they will be able to remain pure and in control.

Our society's history negates such an assumption. We have seen time and again that power corrupts, that it is virtually impossible to control by power alone without becoming controlled by it. Yet at various points in history the church itself has fallen into the great error of trying to find its place in the world through demonstrations of dominance. Consequently, we have seen the proliferation of wars fought in the name of Christ, the entrapment in power mongering of the church that was called by Jesus to be a servant in the world. A critical contemporary issue with which Christians wrestle in lands formerly controlled by the communists is the question of how to deal with church leaders who allied themselves with the secret police in order to secure power.

As a contrast to the world's lust for power and control, I want to pay special tribute to Linden and Tim, to whom this book is dedicated. They have taught me the meaning of Christianity more deeply than brilliant theologians. Their sufferings teach what true victory is. In their courage and perseverance they exhibit more strength than most men caught up in their own macho.

Think what would happen if we would get this straight in our churches: victory is won through sacrifice. Could we aspire to have not the most beautiful church building in the city, but one that provides shelter for the homeless and meals for the hungry? How could our church communities invest ourselves more deeply in the lives of the poor and the dispossessed to teach them skills, to help them find health care and jobs? How can Christians secure land and potential for self-sufficiency for the disenfranchised? What would happen if God's people would truly enter into the situations of our neighbors in order to bring peace and justice to slums, tenement houses, ghettos, the emptiness of riches, the struggles of the physically or mentally disabled?

THE SECOND REASON: THE LAMB WHO SAVES

A pastor friend of mine, for a while unemployed and now ministering to street people, has known poverty from the inside. He has taught me a little of what it means to go hungry, though I recognize the deficiency of being only an observer. We need the dispossessed, the strugglers, the failures, the lonely, the alienated to teach us what it means that the Lamb was slain.

This became much clearer when a graduate school professor struggling with physical limitations grieved with me that no one in the academic ivory tower was able to listen to her pain. It often takes another disabled person truly to stand beside a handicapped person. I'm tired of the "victory, victory—healing and power" heresy that causes those who suffer to feel that they cannot match up to the requirements. Instead, our times of weakness or trials can help us recognize the true meaning of faith in the Suffering Servant.

In Revelation 5 the fact that the Lamb is the one who has been slain calls forth profound adoration on the part of the elders and living creatures. Holding harps and golden bowls of the prayers of the saints (see chapter 20 below), they burst out with a new song proclaiming the worthiness of this slain Lamb to receive the book and to open its seals. He is worthy because in his submission to the slaying he has brought back to God—by virtue of his sacrifice and death—people from every corner of the earth. The song uses a symbolic four to declare that persons from every tribe and tongue and people and nation are thus brought back to God.

Gathering my laundry provides an image for understanding the scriptural use of a symbolic four to indicate the whole world. I collect all the clothes and towels by piling them on top of the bedsheet. Then it is easy to grab all four corners, pull them toward the center, and make a sack out of the sheet to hold everything. In the same way, the ancient use of a symbolic four imagined picking up the whole world by its corners so that nothing earthly was missed. The description in Revelation 5:9, thus, emphasizes that persons from every part of the world were purchased for God by the blood of the slain Lamb.

Once again we must pause before this expression of praise to take stock of the situation in the contemporary church. Could it be that we are not bringing people from every nation because we have lost the essential focus on the one who was slain, rather than on a magical, powerful, super victor? Furthermore, is our evangelism weak because we are not willing to submit our lives to the slaying and sacrifice that make true witness possible? To be followers of Jesus means that we are willing to suffer for others as he did.

The elders and living creatures fall before the mystery of it all. In grateful reverence they acknowledge that this sacrifice is what has enabled the people of God to be a kingdom and priests who will rule on the earth (see also my comments about Rev. 1:6; 3:21; and 20:4). We must take special note of this: our ruling is made possible by his suffering. The church is not to seek power by means of earthly power, but to rule by virtue of Christ's sacrifice for others and our devotion to the Lamb that was slain.

The rest of the chapter records the tremendous crescendo of praise that comes in response to this worthiness. The many angels around the throne who join in this paean of praise number in the thousands upon thousands, the myriads upon myriads. Undoubtedly, these multiples of 10 are meant symbolically, for 10 indicates totality/completion; so the suggestion of totalities times totalities impresses us with the uncountable magnificence of the angelic choir. (I formerly used the word *skillions* to describe it, but then a mathematician friend taught me about googols [10 with 100 zeros behind it] and googolplexes [10^{googol}], numbers that still can't come close to the reality of heavenly praise!) All the creatures of all time and all space resound with a great voice that the slain Lamb is worthy to receive their adoration. All power, wealth, wisdom, strength, honor, glory, and blessing (notice the perfect seven!) belong to him. This song is especially poignant for me because Lutheran liturgies include magnificent settings of these words under the antiphon, "This is the feast of victory for our God." One setting especially uses a constantly running bass on the organ pedals and a majestically marching melody to heighten the awe and splendor of the scene. Every time I sing this part of the liturgy I wish my voice were as great as myriads of trumpets or that I could play a 95-rank organ and hit all the right pedals—but even then my feeble praises would be grossly inadequate.

In verse 13 the praise crescendos once again, as now all the living creatures from the universal four places—the heavens, the earth, under the earth, and the sea—are added to the swelling choir.

Once again they sing a new song, this time with a refrain of these four (universal) elements of attribution: blessing, honor, glory, and dominion belong to him forever and ever (literally, "into the aeons of the aeons"). It will take us all eternity to praise God for his worthiness, and even then we will have just begun.

Those who think heaven will be boring if all we do is sit around playing harps and praising God have never experienced the exquisite pleasure of playing a harp. A friend built for me a lovely 39-string Celtic harp, which delightfully offers endless variations of new things to play. I can hardly imagine that an eternity of praising God could ever be boring. (Maybe I can learn to play the French horn, the cello, and the flute there—and, of course, all the other instruments up there that we haven't even seen yet!)

After this second song of praise in chapter 5 the living creatures cry out, "Amen!"—surely it shall be so!—and fall down once again in reverence and worship. At first this verse seemed redundant, but, as I imagined the scene and thought about the privilege of praising God for his victory through sacrifice, I was filled again with wonder and adoration.

The truth of the scene was profoundly brought home to me once during a horrendously busy time in graduate school when I virtually stopped communicating with my friends far away on the West Coast. I was curt with them and even downright nasty sometimes on the phone, and yet those friends (including the one who is now my husband) continued to love me. What incredible grace! Each time I remember that dreadful month, I am amazed anew. What an unfathomable gift of love—I shall never be able quite to understand its breadth and height. When I multiply that awareness by the googolplexes, I realize I've just begun to imagine the extent of the love manifested in the sacrifice of the Lamb who was slain, and I know that I shall never get tired of learning new songs to praise him. Truly we will say "Amen, Amen" a skillion times and still know that we have barely begun to appreciate that the slain Lamb really has accomplished such a redemption, that he has made us into a kingdom and priests. Will we ever really know what that means? Will we ever get tired of praising him for it? Perhaps we better begin now. My face touches the ground in worship.

17

Don't Forget the First Horse of the Apocalypse!

Please refer often to Revelation 6:1–7:8 and 19:11–21 as you study this chapter.

There was enough nuclear stuff in our world to blow it up entirely at least 35 times. (It seems to me that once is more than enough!) When I first wrote this chapter, leaders of the world were gathering in a conference concerning chemical weapons. It was scary to think of what could happen if some of them got out of control. Wars raged in many parts of the earth—civil war in Mozambique, the Palestinian *intifada*, conflict in Northern Ireland, the Khmer Rouge devastation of Cambodian peasants, the intervention of Contras against Sandinistas in Nicaragua, and civil war in El Salvador—to name just a few that were taking place when I first wrote this chapter. The devastation was enormous; the cost in human lives, outrageous.

And now there is economic chaos. The U.S., with its massive national debt, has become the largest debtor nation in the world. Many third world countries pay more in interest on their loans than they can afford, so they go more and more deeply into arrears. The former Soviet Union is in an economic shambles because of the devastating cost to the peoples there of previously maintaining the arms race. With poorly maintained infrastructures, the communist experiment did not provide means for transporting and preserving harvests, so the people suffer from hunger. Meanwhile, the world used to spend an amount on military equipment in one day equal to the cost of feeding, clothing, and housing the entire world for a year. New weapons continue to be constructed to destroy, while 40,000 people die each day of malnutrition and related diseases. The cost in human lives is outrageous.

And then there is the plague of AIDS. As I write, there has not yet been found a cure for this inevitably terminal illness. Scientists project a huge epidemic of it in the U.S., and already it is the leading cause of death for women between the ages of 25 and 34 in New York City. AIDS has touched us all. The epidemic is scary. We wonder if we will be infected, perhaps from blood received in a transfusion or when we are caring for an AIDS patient.

How can we face this world's situation, with wars, economic chaos, and epidemics facing us on every side? What does it mean to be a Christian in all this mess?

It seems that everybody has heard of the four horses of the apocalypse, but few have paid enough attention to the white horse and its rider. The original readers of The Revelation faced the same three terrifying enemies that we do—wars, economic disasters, and epidemics/deaths—and the seer wrote to comfort them in the face of all these terrors with the assurance that these three forces alone do not control the development of history.

Do not forget: there are four horses in Revelation 6, and the white one reappears in chapter 19. Do not forget that the central message of the whole book is that Jesus is Lord—over the entire cosmos!

We see here for the first time the interlocking patterns of The Revelation (see further exposition in chapters 20 and 22). The opening of the seven seals begins with the four horses and ends with an awesome silence throughout the heavens (8:1). It is important to grasp a larger view of this series than can be gained by focusing simply on the horses themselves. They are part of a greater picture that includes also the sealing of the saints and profound worship by all who observe. These other aspects of the seals remind us that the three horses—war, money, and death—do not have the last word in history. Their machinations and manipulations do not threaten God's sovereignty.

It is also significant that the white horse appears first. In Greek, as in most languages, the places of emphasis are at the beginning and at the end. We don't put the most important things in the middle where they might get lost. In the sequence of the seven seals, the white horse comes first, and the adoration of all of heaven comes last. These symbols of God's sovereignty frame the other elements of the series.

Although some scholars debate the meaning of the white horse, it seems to me very clear that its rider is the Christ. Several elements of the description make this interpretation most conclusive. First of all, the four horses are all introduced by one of the creatures saying, "Come!" However, only the creature who announces the white horse has a voice like thunder—forms of which are used in descriptions all over the place in The Revelation. This brief list helps us to see its thrust:

> *"Thunder," in 14:2, where it describes the voice from heaven, while the seer looked at the Lamb that was slain and the 144,000 he had sealed.*

> *"Thunderings," in 4:5; 8:5; 11:19; and 19:6, which relate to the throne of God, the actions of God, the temple of God, and the people of God, respectively.*

> *"Thunders," in 10:3–4, related to the messages of God spoken by an angel (which the seer was not permitted to record); and 16:18, where the thunders occur when the seventh angel of God dumps out the bowl of weather disasters as the city of Babylon is destroyed.*

Furthermore, the picture of the white horse and its rider reoccurs in chapter 19, and there many of the details convince us that the rider is Christ. We will discuss that portrait more thoroughly at the end of this chapter, but here we must note this crowning title rendered him in chapter 19: King of kings and Lord of lords. Applying that title to the same rider in chapter 6 reminds us that, though other forces in the world seem to be in control, still Christ is Lord over all. None of these other forces can get out of the hand of God's sovereignty.

The other forces are awful indeed. Certainly the fiery red horse of war has dominated history. Jesus warned us of that when he said that there would be wars and rumors of wars until the end of the age. These are not the signs of the end; they are the signs of the times. Throughout the history of fallen humankind there have been wars and rumors of wars. They keep reminding us that this is not God's plan for the world, that human beings have violated his designs and continue to destroy his creation. Contrary to those who think that a nuclear war might usher in the end of time, this text suggests that the fiery horse of war must be kept distinct from the plan of God. Human beings slay each other. God certainly never intended his world to be at war!

The black horse of economic disorder comes next. (Though not its intention in The Revelation, the horse's color painfully reminds me that minority peoples in the U.S. suffer disproportionately from the economic injustice of our society.) The voice among the living creatures tells us how bad it is—that one can only get a small amount of wheat or barley for a day's wages. This is certainly true in many poverty-stricken lands today. The final command not to damage the oil and wine suggests that only God's sovereignty prevents the world from being entirely overwhelmed by economic disaster.

The fourth seal discloses the pale horse of Death and Hades. These forces have caused destruction (limited to a fourth of the earth, 6:8) by means of sword, famine, plague, and the wild beasts of the earth. If we modernized the first three of those four (symbolizing everything earthly) destructive elements, would we list racial riots, welfare cutbacks, or AIDS? And I wonder what we would call contemporary "wild beasts."

The fifth seal (6:9–11) is such an important interruption of this scene of the four horses that we will save its explication for the following chapter.

The sixth seal gives a typical description of the terrors that will appear when God comes. Biblical descriptions for a theophany (i.e., the coming of God) are used—images from Sinai and Egypt—but our focus is immediately drawn to the people who flee from God's appearing.

The description includes all of the earth's powerful—the kings, the great men, the commanders, the rich, the strong, the free men— with only one word signifying the humble: the slave. Certainly the list illustrates that people from all walks of life will flee from God's wrath, but the proportion of words might also indicate that the power and wealth of the mighty make them more susceptible to trusting themselves rather than turning to God.

Immediately after the record of their fleeing and seeking shelter (the description of which again utilizes many passages from the First Testament, which you might enjoy looking up in commentaries or cross-reference Bibles), the text moves to the sealing of God's people, the 144,000. God will not bring his destructive wrath on the earth (or on the sea or the trees either) until his people are made secure.

The list given in 7:5–8 is certainly intended to be symbolic. It begins with Judah, who was not the oldest son of Jacob (and therefore is never named first in the Hebrew lists), but who was the forefather of the tribe from which the Savior came, so there is a notion of grace implied in the list. Second, the list does not include Dan, most likely to emphasize that the horrendousness of that tribe's sins kept them out of God's purposes.

However, there must be 12 tribes of 12,000 each to emphasize that all of God's people are there—especially since a thousand is composed of the number of completion (10) multiplied by itself the divine number (3) of times. Consequently, the number is made complete by including in the list both Joseph (v. 8) and Manasseh (v. 6), Joseph's son.

The list emphasizes that it is not by birthright (since the list doesn't follow the ordering in the Hebrew Scriptures of the 12 sons of Israel) nor by accomplishment (they are sealed by God) that anyone is preserved from the destruction of God's wrath. Only by grace are we part of the elect, the number of which is certainly not limited to 144,000, as we shall see in the following chapter.

Now we can return to the white horse (6:2), riding out as a conqueror bent on a war of conquest. In chapter 19 we meet this horse and rider doing just that, and there is no doubt that the rider is Christ. He is called (in 19:11, 13, and 16) the Word of God (an appellation that links us to the portrait at the beginning of the gospel of John), the Faithful (used in 1:5) and True (names that remind us of his character and draw us into deeper trust), and the King of kings and Lord of lords (titles that speak of the power and authority that he is about to demonstrate).

What is most important for us to note about the final war (19:19) is that it isn't a war. In contrast to all the interpretations of The Revelation that paint lurid scenes of the end of the world, the text says simply that all the kings of the earth who had assembled to make war against Christ were killed with the sword that came out of his mouth. The beast and the false prophet, who have deceived all the people into worshiping the demonic powers, are thrown into the lake of fire, and the dragon himself, the devil or Satan, is thrown into the abyss (20:1–3). When he is released after the 1,000 years for a short time, he will try again to deceive the nations and gather them together for war, but once again they will be easily dispensed with (and by no human effort). Fire from heaven will devour all the nations, and the devil will be thrown into the lake of fire along with the beast and false prophet (vv. 7–10).

In other words, the final end of evil will be easily accomplished because, as recorded in other places (such as Col. 2:14–15) as well as The Revelation, Christ has already conquered the principalities and powers at the cross and empty tomb. He is already King of kings and Lord of lords.

This is underscored by the fact that in Revelation 6 Christ rides out with the other three horses as influences upon history, but, in the end, he is the only one to ride out. Other forces of history— other rulers and authorities—might think they are having a great influence, but their truly feeble power is dismissed with one or two verses. The rider of the white horse, on the other hand, comes again to conquer ultimately and to save.

Since he is King of kings and Lord of lords already, what does that mean for our suffering? How we can live in the light of this fact is the subject of the next chapter.

18

Endurance: The Meaning of Biblical Patience

Please refer to Revelation 6:9–11 and 7:9, 13–15 as you study this chapter.

All pain remedies promise faster relief than their competitors, and all problems in TV situation comedies are solved in only half an hour. Surely we live in an age of instant fixes and gratifications. Tragically, even Christians who become more and more enculturated easily fall into attitudes that demand instant spiritual gratification.

That is why I have chosen these two texts from consecutive chapters of The Revelation to illustrate the biblical concept of patience (though that word is not used in these passages). The people of the church at Ephesus were commended for their perseverance, as were the folks from Thyatira (see 2:2–3 and 19). In those places the Greek word *hupomone* is used. Understanding this word properly is essential for a biblical theology of weakness.

The original Greek word is composed of the preposition *hupo*, which means "below," and *mone*, which comes from the verb meaning "to remain." The biblical concept of *hupomone* carries this connotation of being able to remain under or continuing to bear up under difficult circumstances—not just a patience until things change, but a remaining-under perseverance made possible by the knowledge that the Lord stands with us.

When I pray in the midst of the frustrations of chronic illness, I cannot pray only to have patience until God changes my body and makes everything easy. If that is what I expect, then I would have run out of patience long ago. Rather, biblical patience means to bear up—even if the situation never changes, even if it becomes worse—because God is there in the midst of the anguish to comfort and to guide and to continue his work of healing.

How precious this concept is when we minister to those with physical challenges or struggle with them ourselves! I do believe that at times God grants miraculous healing—and that we do not ask for his interventions enough. However, in many situations we are left with the "thorn in the flesh." How then can we understand the Lord's sovereignty? If he is all powerful and good, why doesn't he heal?

Theologians have wrestled with that question ever since Job, and it is probably not to our best purposes here to hash through all the answers. However, it is critically important for us to note the lesson that these sections from The Revelation can teach us about biblical patience.

Notice that when the fifth seal is broken (6:9–11) the ones having been slaughtered and waiting beneath the altar cry out to ask how long, but they are not given the answer that they would soon be delivered. Rather, they are told that they must wait while others would be martyred also. Their fellow servants, their brothers and sisters, too, were going to be killed.

As we skip ahead to the next chapter of The Revelation, we see these same persons from the other side, after the time of persecution is complete. In 7:9 they are the ones who gather before the throne of the Lamb, dressed in white robes and carrying palms of victory in their hands.

The symbolism of this picture is probably familiar to all of us— white robes, signifying purity and victory, and palm branches, used even as they were on Palm Sunday to welcome the king with royal splendor. Furthermore, the text uses the symbolic number four to describe the groups out of which these saints came—from every ethnic group and nation and people and language.

Remember our illustration (in the previous chapter) of the symbolic four and my laundry? This description, then, emphasizes that persons from every part of the earth are included in the multitude of the saints who have washed their robes and made them white. Such groupings of fours are often used throughout the Scriptures, but especially in The Revelation, to emphasize the universality of it all, to remind us that the whole world or every earthly possibility is represented in the collection.

In Revelation 7:10 the saints rightfully acknowledge that salvation belongs to God. The passage underscores the point once again that they are not being regarded for their expertise in being faithful, but that God is faithful to give them the gift of the crown of life.

After another song with seven elements (7:12) and the customary refrains ("forever and ever, Amen"), the text uses an element typical in prophetic literature. The elder asks the seer the question, "Who are the ones clothed in white robes, and from where do they come?" Such a device is used to heighten interest in the answer to the question. The seer responds that he is ignorant by asserting instead that the angel who asked the question knows.

The angel's answer to his own question is accentuated by a difference in verb forms that highlights the hope we have in our suffering. When the text says that they have washed their robes and made them white, the verbs are decisive, once-for-all verbs. The action of becoming dressed with the garments of salvation is a decisive, once-for-all event.

Coming through the tribulation, on the other hand, is a process in which the seer John himself was participating. The use of a present tense verb for "saints who come" gives us confidence that someday we, too, will join those saints who have arrived at the other side. We have, indeed, already washed our robes and become dressed in the garments of salvation, but that does not mean that our problems are automatically ended. The Lamb justifies us and creates our relationship with him in the washing of the robes, and the hope of eventually coming through the tribulation gives us courage for living in it.

The text says that these who are coming out of the great tribulation, which probably meant in the original setting of The Revelation that they had suffered at the hands of the emperor, are right now serving the Lord day and night in his temple. Moreover, someday the one who dwells on the throne will tabernacle upon them. This passage underscores the already-but-not-yet-ness of God's promises. Already to some extent God's kingdom has come to our world, but not yet has God fully tabernacled upon us. The promise of his thorough tabernacling—his total reign—is still to be fulfilled.

A very exciting biblical concept is introduced by the word-*tabernacle* in Revelation 7:15. It reveals a vital aspect of a theology of weakness.

To understand its use completely, think about God's tabernacling (or the way in which he pitches his tent) in three different verb tenses: past, present, and future. Three important passages guide our consideration of these terms. In the *past*, "the Word became flesh and tabernacled among us" (a literal translation of John 1:14). At a particular point in history, this most amazing thing occurred: God himself became as one of us and pitched his tent in our midst. The text goes on to say that when God so entered into our situation, we humans were able for the first time to behold God's glory, full of grace and truth. We saw it in the person of Jesus, as he "pitched his tent" and lived a fully human (yet thoroughly divine) existence among us.

Now here in Revelation 7, we read that someday God will pitch his tent among us again. The verb is a *future* tense verb—he hasn't yet tabernacled totally among us, for this world still remains and saints still come through persecutions. Rather, it is a promise of hope for the early Christians and for us. Someday God himself will manifestly dwell in our midst.

The verb's *present* tense use is especially significant for our purposes here, for how God can tabernacle upon us in the present is a concept full of surprises. We read about it in Paul's second letter to the Corinthians.

In the 12th chapter of that book, Paul describes his suffering from the thorn in the flesh. In three periods of asking the Lord to remove that thorn he received the answer (v. 9) that God's grace was sufficient for all his needs. The next phrase, a thorough exegetical study reveals, could perhaps be better translated than the usual "my power is made perfect in weakness." The Greek verb translated "made perfect" is the verb *teleo*, which in every other place in the New Testament is translated "brought to the finish." The verb that would be translated "made perfect" is the slightly expanded verb *teleioo*. Significantly, the simpler verb is used in this place. Furthermore, there is no pronoun "my" in the original Greek text. Therefore, the phrase could instead be translated, "for power is brought to its end in weakness." Then Paul's next sentence would logically follow: "All the more gladly, accordingly, will I glory rather in my weakness, in order that the power of Christ [instead of my own feeble power which has ended] will take up residence/tabernacle in me!"

The translation "power is brought to its end in weakness" underscores more clearly why grace is sufficient for us in thorny times. When we give up our own feeble power and let it be finished in weakness, then God's grace can work more thoroughly on us, and in us, and through us. As long as we are capable of doing things on our own, we never thoroughly realize the power of God at work in us. However, when weakness makes us incapable of doing what we would like to do, then we no longer struggle out of our feeble power. Then God can conform us to his will. Then we are a submitted vessel in his hands.

All of this leads up to the point of this chapter on the biblical concept of patience, for Paul says next (2 Cor. 12:9b) that he will all the more gladly boast about his weakness because then the power of God tabernacles upon him. In this instance, the verb "to tabernacle" includes the preposition *epi* added to the front of it. *Epi* means "approaching towards or upon" something, so the verb stresses that God indeed tabernacles in us. We miss his tabernacling presence and power when we obstruct him with our own efforts. We are never quite weak and dependent enough; our sinful natures want to accomplish our salvation by our own efforts. However, when we can acknowledge and live from our weakness, God tabernacles upon us!

Thus, just as Jesus once came and tabernacled among us in the human form of his incarnation (John 1:14), and just as God will someday perfectly tabernacle among us at the Last Day (Rev. 7:15), even so he tabernacles upon us now in our weakness! And when our power is brought to its finish, we will learn the sufficiency of God's grace and the powerful presence of his dwelling in us.

This biblical concept throws overboard the whole modern emphasis on winning and being number one and having power. Greatly to our surprise, it is not in our sufficiency or capability that God can tabernacle among us. It is in our weakness. In our failures, in the times when we are suffering or coming through great tribulations, we can best experience his presence.

The implications of this concept are enormous. Whereas modern society tends to be impressed with big buildings, refined television productions, and lots of pizzazz, the truth of God's tabernacling invites us to enter instead into homeless shelters, refugee camps, convalescent centers, ghettos, soup kitchens, prisons, and homes for the insane and retarded. By participating in the suffering of those who are weak, we learn the sufficiency of God's grace.

For example, I think often of Clifford, who suffered from muscular dystrophy and yet who served all the people around him in the convalescent center that was his home. Whenever I came with my guitar to sing for patients, he would direct me to the rooms of specific people who needed special attention, and he knew in each case which hymns were their favorites.

Or I think of my swimming friend Perry. One day in the pool, I was on the verge of tears from the pain and from trying to face how much my body has deteriorated since the days when I was a competitive swimmer. I asked Perry how he could keep going on, and he answered with his customary gentle kindness, encouraging me not to give up altogether. And Perry has only one arm!

Similarly, my friends Linden and Tim often usher me into the presence of God. Sometimes I even imagine that God's tabernacle sits around their wheelchair and dialysis machine.

In a technological society that emphasizes strength and efficiency and, therefore, has little patience, the Christian community has great gifts to offer in our recognition of the sufficiency of grace in weakness and in our care for those who suffer. By pointing to the tabernacling of God in weakness we can encourage and honor those in our midst who are enduring various kinds of tribulation. By inviting them to teach classes or to give witness in a worship service, we could make better use of the gifts and awarenesses of those who have known God's presence most deeply in their limitations. All of us need to understand more deeply a patience that does not wait for things to change, but which recognizes instead that "remaining under" is the way to find the presence of God in new ways.

When I was first struggling with the permanent (but not eternal!) crippling of my left leg, many well-intentioned people kept asking if my foot was better, even though I had already deliberately told them that the bones had healed crookedly. Their frequent question made me feel not acceptable because I was not making progress. The situation made me aware that many who suffer from chronic illness or worsening handicaps suffer even more from the comments of those who want an instant fix. Instead, let us find ways in our Christian communities to encourage those with physical challenges to rejoice in their limitations as extra opportunities for learning about the sufficiency of God's grace and the power of his tabernacling.

When we remember in our Christian communities the biblical concept of patience, we are better able to care for those with various kinds of struggles, debilitating handicaps, mental or emotional disabilities, and chronic diseases. We will more effectively support them if, as they endure circumstances that might not change, we can point to our God, who still tabernacles. As we participate together in sufferings and face the challenges of weaknesses, we will all learn what it truly means to be patient because God dwells with us.

19

The Third Reason for Praise: Hope for the Future

Please refer often to Revelation 7:9–17 as you study this chapter.

Over the course of the past 20 years, I have experienced periods of deep grieving because of physical or emotional/spiritual set-backs—both of which raise the question of the justice of God. Life sometimes hardly seems fair. Why should I have to suffer? The question was more painful before my marriage, for I struggled alone, without anyone to help me as more and more the complications of brittle diabetes took their toll on my nerves and bones and eyes and metabolic system. God sometimes seems so cruel when he allows such evil and suffering to exist in the world.

There are no easy answers. Theologians offer various perspectives and never thoroughly solve the mystery. Meanwhile, we live in a world marred by sin and ignorance. God's plan for his creation is thwarted time and again. Sometimes we even must be willing to *choose* to suffer to be faithful to biblical principles. It all seems unfair; the pain at times threatens to drown us.

In the midst of our despair the seventh chapter of The Revelation offers us tremendous hope. Not only does it picture the eventual triumph of the saints who experienced terrible sufferings and yet came through the tribulation, but this chapter also gives us the third major reason for praise: that someday our tears, too, will end, and suffering will be gone forever. Certainly we all look forward to that day with eager anticipation. Surely we are all too tired of all the pain in this world. So many people have sufferings beyond their ability to cope. Everything seems so out of control.

There is an immense danger in all the world's pain of oversimplifying the text before us, of merely saying that we can endure what troubles we have now because someday God will take us away from this vale of tears to a place where there is only Joy. To look *only* to the future without acknowledging the pain of the present is to dump an empty gospel on those who suffer. Christians misused such a line to keep the blacks in slavery for a long time!

I hate that kind of canned comfort that merely pats us on the back and says, "Wait till heaven and then all will be better." Such a response doesn't begin to touch the depth of pain in people's suffering. It is cruel to ignore someone's present anguish by simply insisting that when we get to heaven it will be better. "Pie in the sky in the bye and bye when we die" does not truly help us cope with the endless round of struggles and woes in this life.

So how can this page from The Revelation help? The secret lies in grasping with patience (see my previous chapter) that the eternal has already begun with God's sealing assurance. Eternal hope isn't merely pie in the sky. Rather, God lets us taste it here in the gift of his seal and his presence.

Tim said once, "God makes me so happy right now that I can't imagine life being even better after I die." Since he said that with two huge needles stuck into his arm for the kidney dialysis that keeps him alive, the poignancy of the moment strikes me whenever I begin to complain about tears in my life.

In the beginning of Revelation 7, the seer is told the number of those who have the seal of God on their foreheads: 12,000 from each of the 12 tribes. The repetition of the number 12,000 12 times reminds us forcefully that *all* the people of God will be sealed since 12 always stands for the people of God and 1,000 is the number of completion (10) multiplied by itself a divine (3) number of times. Certainly such divinely complete chosenness emphasizes powerfully that all of God's people will be sealed!

The fact that we are sealed is recorded in the Greek perfect tense, which means that once God's people are decisively sealed this guarantee remains in effect. Moreover, the deliberate listing of the tribes' names and numbers underscores that God specifically knows his people—he knows them each by name, Jesus told us—but it is a symbolic number and list to emphasize that the crowd is greater than can really be imagined. A seal in biblical times (as well as ours) indicates the security of any official document—the authenticity, ownership, and protection of the one who imprints his seal.

This mark of assurance gives us comfort in the meanwhile as we await the fulfillment of God's promise to take away all our tears.

As we wrestle with various problems in our lives, we realize again and again that our deepest needs are those that are satisfied by the present sealing of God. We long for the authenticating support of a God who values us, who urges us in his Word to do what we are capable of doing but sometimes doubt, who will stand beside us in the hard times. We ardently desire the commitment of a God who owns us, not in the nasty sense of fate or coercion, but in the loving sense of providing for all our needs and making it possible for us to become all that he designed us to be. We yearn for the security of being protected, especially if we face continued struggle with physical or emotional ailments. All these things are hinted at by the seal of God.

At various points in life, we agonize over such trials as aloneness, the limitations of handicaps, the frustrations and failures of community and vocation and family life. If we keep things on the surface, if we ignore the reality of present suffering, and instead comfort each other merely with glib statements that someday all will be better, we fail to offer the very resource that should be most helpful in our sufferings. In fact, sometimes the comfort that Christians unwittingly offer each other is frighteningly destructive.

The fact that the end of Revelation 7 asserts that someday the saints will not hunger or thirst anymore or that the sun will not beat down on them indicates that now they might be suffering from hunger or thirst or heat exhaustion. Our solace to others must acknowledge in a healthy tension both sides of this dialectical reality: the future freedom from the present struggles. Contrary to our expectations that life should be easier, the fact is that we will most likely continue to suffer in this present world.

The theology of weakness that dominates The Revelation provides a way to keep both sides of the dialectic in balance. As one who himself suffered, the seer John offered visions of hope to those in tribulation. The experience of struggles teaches us what kind of comfort really ministers to those newly entering into pain or blindingly stymied by its constant proliferation.

The best way we can help each other in the suffering is to acknowledge its existence as an indelible part of our existence in a world marred by sin and human destructiveness—to lament with the psalms over the seeming absence of God. We are better enabled to fight the effects of sin if we are able to acknowledge its bitter reality more thoroughly. Then we are not so surprised and thwarted by the failure of our efforts to change things. Then we are able to keep on being faithful because the failures don't daunt us. We know they occur in an evil world where pain is inevitable.

Nevertheless, this requires a very careful tension. We can easily fall off the other side of the tightrope into the pit of despair. If pain and suffering are always going to be the case, then why work so hard to change them?

This chapter's text provides us with the balance necessary to avoid slipping into despair. Those who have passed through the tribulation assure us that indeed someday the pain will be no more. Someday the tears will be wiped away forever. Meanwhile, as we wait for that day, we can taste of that possibility in the various fleeting moments of victory that we experience now. Learning to delight in those moments, not expecting them to last very long, we know they merely whet our appetite for the ultimate victory.

Thus, another factor in our remaining hopeful is a constant recognition that we are but strangers and sojourners here. This is not the real life for which we are destined. Someday, things are going to be different, according to God's perfect plan. Though we know very little about the future heaven or what happens after death, the point is that God's promise is not just an illusion. Someday things *will* be different; evil *will* be destroyed. The vision of saints participating in that future strengthens our hope for it now.

I celebrated a moment of that present future at my grandmother's funeral. She was 94 when she died and had suffered pain and weakness and loss of physical and mental capacities for many years. Yet she had always been able to pray with me in German, and I enjoyed reading Scripture lessons and devotions to her in her native tongue. My uncle reported that her homegoing was wonderful. After reciting German hymns and prayers for a long time (in a clear, firm voice, though earlier in the day she'd only mumbled), suddenly she said in English, "And that's all I know"—her last words before she died. What more does one need to know besides hymns of praise and prayers of trust?

After the funeral home visitation, the pastor read Revelation 7 to the family members. Since I had been immersed in that text for this book, its imagery moved me profoundly. My heart soared as I pictured Grandmother, wearing her white robe, free to praise God as he is worthy to be praised (in German, of course!) and no longer suffering any pain or limitations. The ecstasy of that vision lifted me from the pain of my newly shattered foot. I cried with Joy as I exulted in my heart, "No more tears, liebe Grossmutter!"

This is always the emphasis of biblical eschatology (the consideration of the endtimes). The Scriptures hold in tension the already and the not-yet. We already experience the grace of God, but it is only a foretaste of his perfect presence, which is not yet realized. Someday the tears will be gone, and the assurance of the fulfillment of that promise enables us to cry less now.

We know that someday the Lamb will thoroughly shepherd us because to some extent we experience his tenderness now. Every time we have felt that we absolutely could not go on, somehow a moment of his grace slipped in to assure us of his loving care. The Christian life is composed of looking to those moments as foretastes of God's complete restoration, a recognition that already the tending has begun, even though we don't experience it fully now.

Certainly we are not able to maintain this dialectical balance of the present and future without doubts here and there. Indeed, perhaps many of the tears that God will someday wipe away forever are tears of despair from the times when we just cannot believe his promises to us and tears of anger against him from the times when life seems so unfair and out of control.

Meanwhile, in the moments when there are no answers, perhaps we will come closer to being able to live with the questions themselves. For example, since my marriage I have been constantly overwhelmed by the goodness of God that he gave me such a gentle husband in Myron, whose tender care makes the questions of my physical limitations so much easier to bear. In our moments of wrestling with pain and human confusion, we will surely see the grace of God in new ways—as today, when the vision of new spring flowers lifted for a while my apprehension as I wait for biopsy of newly found tumors. Sometimes the mere apprehension of that grace will dry our tears for the day.

I believe this even when I can't feel it. I experience it when I focus on serving God instead of on myself. And that takes us back to the necessity for theocentrism with which we began this book. As long as we focus on our own misery and our own questions about why God allows things to be as awful as they sometimes are, our perspectives get jaundiced and inward-turned. Then we wind up miserable in our groping.

On the other hand, when we let our perspective be theocentric, when we declare with the living creatures of The Revelation that God is worthy to receive the blessing, the glory, the wisdom, the thanksgiving, the honor, the power, and the might into the aeons of the aeons, then we can be content to believe that we don't have all the information yet. We can't come to any reasoned conclusions when all the data is not yet in our hands. We don't know how God will take care of us in the future, what he will show us about our troubled existence, how he will enable us to cope with whatever has to be, how he will use our struggles and suffering to bring blessings not only to ourselves, but also to others in the process. We just don't know enough yet *not* to trust him.

I wrote that last line with great deliberation, because it seems that our problem lies in trying to work everything out the other way around. We won't trust God unless he proves himself, and in the course of our demanding that he prove himself we probably miss most of the data that would convince us. If, on the other hand, we could be more open to how God will work through our situations for his very best purposes, we might be more able to wait for his revelation and timing and control.

I write this with great trembling, for many times I cannot believe it. In the moments when I do, however, I am sure that the Christian community needs to be enfolding itself in this message of finding God's presence in our weakness. As Tim once said to me, "I don't even want to be well if that is not God's best for me." I pray that I will grow to be more able to trust the seal with which I am marked, too. I don't know enough yet *not* to trust God.

20

Skills to Read The Revelation: Silence and Trust in God's Vindication

Please refer often to Revelation 8 as you study this chapter.

One especially wonderful aspect of Lutheran liturgies is that they include an occasional pause for silence within the structure of the worship services, but in my frequent travels to teach I have rarely participated in any congregations that really observed the silence. That disappoints me, because moments for reflection provide wonderful opportunities for the surprises of God.

Why do we have such a difficult time being silent? Our culture does not teach us how to enjoy periods of silence. Both psychologists and sociologists have commented on the "noise" of modern culture, the need to have the radio or television set always on. They usually link that need to an inability to live with our own thoughts, to be reflective or creative. The noise and busy-ness of our entertainment culture contrast with the biblical call to meditation, to stillness before God.

Sometimes what we fear in the silence is the pain of a confrontation with ourselves. What sorts of thoughts might come to us and force us to face up to mistakes and failures? In the silence of despair we might hear the accusing voice of the Slanderer making us feel guilty about things that actually have been forgiven. Perhaps in the silence we find it difficult to distinguish between the voice of God telling us things that we need to acknowledge and confess and the voice of Satan trying to upset us and stymie our ministries.

One evening when I was first writing this book, something that my hostess and I had discussed earlier in the evening touched off a whole barrage of painful memories that kept me from working for a long time. I couldn't settle back into serious thinking until I could sort things through. However, even as I went to sleep that night after prayers, those thoughts were still there to be wrestled with. How can our silences be productive and good?

Because of that question I am intrigued by the half hour of silence that begins the eighth chapter of The Revelation. What a fascinating interlude! What did the seer John experience in that time? What would happen in our worship services if we stopped for half an hour to meditate without sound?

This phenomenal quiet in the seer's vision is not explained. Were the heavens mute because no one was quite ready to cope with the immensity of the vision's events? Was the silence generated by great gratitude for the previous promise that the Lamb will someday wipe away all tears from every eye and lead all the saints to fountains of living water? Or was the quiet a hushed anticipation of the things to come? And what is the connection of this silence with the next event, the channeling of the prayers of the saints to God, or to the following event, the preparation of the angels to sound their trumpets and initiate the plagues of hail and fire to consume part of the earth?

We cannot know for sure with what the silence should be connected, but it seems likely that we should relate it to all the preceding and following aspects of the heavenly vision. Silence is an important element of praise, thanksgiving, awe, fear, reverence, dread, repentance, anticipation, prayer. In our busy lives, silence offers great gifts for our relationship with God.

Besides offering the heavenly model of silence for our lives and worship, the very lack of information about the silence in this text also invites us to learn skills for reading the Bible carefully and meditatively. Obviously, this volume is not a commentary. I haven't offered rigid identifications of every symbol nor much specific factual information about the book of Revelation. I have written very little in this book that you could not have figured out for yourself, given enough time and meditation. My point is that what we need most to do to deepen our biblical literacy is to learn to read the Scriptures carefully both by ourselves and in discussion groups.

Too much we depend on scholars or pastors to give us all the answers, to tell us what we should know about the Scriptures. Certainly the clergy are specially trained to help laypersons grow in skills and to give them information they wouldn't have the time or expertise to dig out for themselves. However, they are not necessarily any better at listening to God than someone who hasn't gone to a seminary. In fact, sometimes those of us who are theologically trained are less able to hear what God is saying because we throw up all sorts of intellectualizing barriers to the Spirit's movement. One of the things I fear most about graduate theological education is that too much learning often takes people away from the major lesson of this book—that in weakness, in our lack of human wisdom and answers, come the best dependence on God and ultimately the victory of faith.

Those who have theological education have acquired it in order that they might be more faithful to their call to be "equipping the saints" (Eph. 4:12). However, that is no more important a station in life than that of the saint who continues to minister to others while working in a factory or office. All of us are ministers together, sharing in our communities the work of the kingdom. We each contribute our part to the building up of the whole. My work as a specially trained layperson is to learn as much as I can in my studies so that I can be as helpful as possible to other saints through Bible lectures and books, but I am painfully aware that I certainly don't know God as well as those who live and walk with him in gentle simplicity.

This sidetrack intends to emphasize that The Revelation is not a book for specialists. In fact, the specialists often miss its point. If they try to pin everything down and to have all the answers for what each item in the text represents, they might miss the whole point of the book: to learn the meaning of Christ's lordship for our times of tribulation and sufferings.

That is especially manifested by this text about silence. No one can say for sure why this particular silence for this length of time and in this context occurred at this point in the heavenly vision. No one can pin down those specifics. However, all of us can meditate on this text and recognize in it a heavenly model that could fittingly be applied to our earthly worship.

Long ago when I first participated in a silent retreat, I panicked at the beginning because it seemed that the long silence would be too painful for me. Too many previous nights had overflowed with tears because of various troubles, so I was not sure I could handle all the hours of silence at the retreat.

To my great surprise, as soon as I left the retreat house for a long walk up the hill and through the fields, my spirit soared with an exquisite Joy. I found myself dancing all over the hillside, singing songs with my hands, and grinning from ear to ear. What an amazing morning—such an amazing grace!

When we came in for lunch, what should be playing as background music but Pachelbel's "Canon in D," which is for me the consummate picture of God's steadfast grace! The same eight notes in the bass line repeat over and over without any variation or change (just like God's love), while the texture up above in the violins and cellos keeps changing magnificently. No matter what music our lives weave above, the *cantus firmus* of God's protective and enveloping grace remains constant and faithful! "Canon in D" epitomized what I had been experiencing all morning in the silence. God did not leave me alone to weep during those hours. He came to me in the sunshine and field flowers, in the spring breezes and birdsongs, in the music and smiles of my retreat partners, and, most of all, in his Word, to fill me with an abundance of Joy that I can't begin to describe adequately.

Moments of silence give opportunities for our reflections on the Scriptures in order to give way to the Spirit's teaching and inspiration. God enables us to understand the Bible much more deeply when there is plenty of time for God's work in our minds, the renewal that is the Holy Spirit's gift. Also, silence helps us to give God the reverence he deserves. As Habakkuk urges, "The LORD is in his holy temple; let all the earth be silent before him" (Hab. 2:20 NASB). In our busy-ness we do not experience the awesomeness of his holiness; in the silence we breathe in the magnificence that cannot be uttered.

Silence also gives us opportunity to observe, to listen, to be made more aware of all that surrounds us—the ways in which God acts in our environment and intervenes in our history, as well as the methods of evil in our world. We need to think more deeply about those principalities and powers that we must fight and about how to combat them. If we try to fight evil without adequate reflection and preparation, our actions are often ill-founded or unsuitable to the actual situation. If we give ourselves meditative space and time to understand God's Word, we can more accurately apply the truths of God to the circumstances we encounter. Our most important model is Jesus, who frequently retreated to the hills to pray and commune with his Father, especially before such major decisions as choosing the 12 apostles (Luke 6:12–16).

For all these reasons, I think the silence observed in the seer's heavenly vision is not only a response to the joy of chapter 7, but also very closely related to both of the following events in Revelation 8. One special element of style underscores these connections. The text mentions immediately after the silence that seven angels were given trumpets, so the silence may well be meant to prepare us for the agony when those trumpets sound and usher in the destruction of the earth. However, their work does not begin until after the account of the prayers of the saints. This literary construction of interruption and framing, which is also frequently used for emphasis by the gospel writers, here highlights the connection of the silence and the prayers.

The symbolic number seven occurs twice again to emphasize that exactly the perfect number of angels and trumpets will be used for the next stage in God's assertion of his lordship. The term *angel* literally means "messenger," and as they blow their trumpets later in the text we will notice that they function merely to announce the various elements of the destruction. God is therefore seen indirectly to be the cause of the punishment, not venting a petty human vengeance on the enemy, but finally exercising his righteous and long-withheld wrath. In these very acts of asserting his lordship we realize that he has been graciously patient for a long time.

However, these acts of retribution also respond to the prayers of the saints who have suffered extraordinarily at the hands of their enemies. We recognize this connection because the seer John places the angels with trumpets as a frame (8:2 and 6) around the few verses (3–5) that talk about the prayers of the saints, which includes their prayers for vindication (6:9–11).

Another angel appears with the golden censer of prayers. This angel mixes the prayers of the saints together with the smoke of his incense. This scene seems to represent the intercession of heavenly forces along with the prayers of God's people. We know from the words of Jesus that he intercedes for us (John 17) and from the apostle Paul that the Holy Spirit intercedes for us (Rom. 8:27). Here in Revelation 8:3 we are reminded of that great fact—that all our prayers are only supplements to those of the angelic hosts, the heavenly beings, and God himself. Moreover, our prayer is connected with the silence and with the action of God's wrath in response to the needs of the saints. We are invited by this scene, therefore, to connect everything in our lives with our prayers—our gratitude for the deliverance from tears promised in the last chapter, our awe at the majesty of God, our desire to be freed from the tormentings of our enemies. All these things are matters for our prayers.

The subject of prayer is much too large for us to pursue thoroughly in this book. However, the beginning of Revelation 8 invites us to enjoy silence in our prayers. Spending time at the listening end of prayer enables us to hear the answers God gives to our intercessions and the purposes he teaches.

The prayers of the saints and the incense having been mingled and received by God, the angel then throws the contents of the censer to earth. This image invites us to faithful diligence in the discipline of prayer, for it suggests graphically that God takes our prayers seriously and causes momentous happenings on earth. Peals of thunder and rumblings and lightnings and earthquakes (notice that there are four elements!) again remind us of Mount Sinai and God's appearance there to instruct his people. Such images here remind us that God does indeed come to us in response to our prayers; his epiphany immediately greets the saints in prayer.

Finally, verse 6 specifically proclaims that the angels prepared themselves in order to sound their trumpets. That line of anticipation increases our expectations and fear, for the trumpets warn of God's impending wrath.

The people of Israel had employed trumpets in their special holiday celebrations and at times to summon the militia together for battle or defense (see, for example, Num. 10:3–10; 29:1). Trumpets were also used in the coronations of kings (as in 1 Kings 1:34, 39; 2 Kings 9:13). At one point in the First Testament they were used to announce God's wrath (Zeph. 1:14–16). The references to trumpets in The Revelation might have brought several of these First Testament images to mind for its first readers. God was indeed asserting his kingship and ushering in a new age. Images of triumph and venting wrath are also appropriate.

As the trumpets sound, various plagues are cast on the earth— fire, hail, blood, a star that turns the waters bitter, and darkness. All of these affect one-third of the earth, the sea, the waters, the light-giving bodies.

As we move through The Revelation, we will notice that its patterns describing the destructions of God's wrath are like a guide in an art gallery as the descriptions continue to restate and enlarge their themes. There is much literary development in the text that does not necessarily represent different stages in the historical outworking of God's final triumph. Rather, we can see considerable circling around in details as chapters 6 through 11 progress. The further one moves towards the final consummation of history, the greater is the enlargement of the details. This literary style makes sense because as we come closer to insight, we can see more thoroughly the nature of the matter at hand. So we can compare Revelation 8:7–13 with 9:1–21, as well as 10:1–11:14, to see the continued spiraling of these restatements in larger terms.

The fact that the book of Revelation must be understood cyclically, as enlarging spheres of literary development, is hinted at in the very beginning, where the letters to the seven churches are arranged in a circle, and particular literary patterns are repeated precisely to show the repetition with variation that characterized God's rebukes (refer again to chapter 7).

Next we move on to various cycles of scenes in heaven and in battles against evil, emphasizing that as long as this world continues such cycles will continue to be a constant process. Ultimately, as we shall see at the end of The Revelation, God will totally destroy all evil, but in the meanwhile, as history repeats itself, human sin cycles around, deserving God's wrath but also calling forth his patient grace. To the specific venting of God's wrath and the immensity of his grace we will turn in later chapters.

21

The Persistence of Sin and the Immensity of Grace

Please refer often to Revelation 8:6–9:21 as you study this chapter.

I first revised this chapter the day after, to my great surprise, my best friend proposed to me. (The discipline of writing was a good way to keep my feet on the ground at least a little.) It was amazing that Myron asked me to marry him after he had faithfully waited through six years of friendship (including my four-year stint across the country for graduate school) and many days of uncertainty about my vocation. Moreover, his proposal came in a time of confusion and concern over a new health complication. In contrast to the usual romantic notions of Prince Charming falling in love with the most beautiful maiden, he proposed when my leg was ugly red and grotesquely swollen. What incredible love! It has to be (as Myron first declared) the work of God.

What wonderful timing that on the day I had planned to write about the immensity of God's grace for a sinful world I should experience its Joy so richly through the gift of Myron! In this overwhelming love I realize that human devotion is just one small taste of the infinite love God has for us.

Most people find the description of the trumpets in the eighth and ninth chapters of The Revelation to be gruesome and weird and horrible. However, if we read carefully, we will see that it is designed to show us—with bizarre imagery, I admit—how immeasurably boundless God's love is.

To see that love, instead of merely being frightened by what at first glance seems to be an awful picture, we must carefully notice some little details. Most important, the accounts of all the trumpets clearly show that God is in control.

148

These chapters of The Revelation raise a difficult issue: how evil in the world relates to God's sovereignty. In this picture, although the forces of evil are unleashed to do their destructive work, they cannot do it until God's angels sound their trumpets. God is not the author of evil, but he is sovereign over it.

God's control is suggested, first of all, by his deliberate confining of the destruction. All the results of the first four trumpets are limited to one-third. Moreover, after these trumpets have sounded and their plagues have wreaked their desolations, an eagle with a loud voice warns the inhabitants of the earth that more of God's trumpets are about to sound.

God's control is even clearer when chapter 9 expands the descriptions of the trumpets. In Revelation 9:3 the seer declares that the locusts were *given* power; they had not usurped it for themselves. Their actions come as the result of the fifth angel sounding his trumpet. God's messenger issued his command, and the locusts were allotted a certain amount of power.

Second, Revelation 9:4 proclaims that their power was specifically limited by restrictions on their actions. The locusts could harm neither the plants of the earth nor the people who had the seal of God on their foreheads, nor were they able to kill anyone. They were given power to inflict pain, but not death. It seems that those people who were not sealed by God were thereby given impetus to think about their lives. In seeking death (but it eludes them, v. 6), they will perhaps think again about the meaning of life.

Now in The Revelation we begin to see—in the case of the star who is given the key to the bottomless pit—the ambiguity of the powers of evil, that their forms sometimes imitate God. Although Christ is called the Morning Star both in Revelation 2:28 and 22:16, and in 3:7 he holds the key, the "star" in 9:1 who wields the key to the abyss is probably not Christ. Rather, it seems likely that this star released by the fifth trumpet is the star called Wormwood, which in Revelation 8:10–11 was released by the third trumpet to fall on the waters and turn them bitter and cause people to die.

Later, in chapters 13 and 14 of The Revelation (which we will discuss in chapter 24 of this book), we will see that the powers of evil imitate the triune God as they wreak their havoc in the world. Similarly, here the star who is given the key to the abyss (but temporarily, since an angel has the key in Rev. 20:1) seems to be a parody of the true Morning Star, who actually holds the keys and who cannot be frustrated (see Rev. 3:7). Evil seems to have its way, but its reality is imitation and under the control of the truth.

This was a crucially important message for the early Christians being persecuted. Because it must have often seemed as if evil was in control, they needed the reminder that God reigned supreme.

The description of the locusts released from the pit (9:7–10) is certainly gruesome, but its strange contrasts again enable us to see that it is symbolically graphic in order to make a point. One certainly couldn't produce an artist's rendition of all the features in this description that would make any sense. However, each detail suggests a factor for our understanding.

First of all, the locusts look like horses prepared for battle. Obviously, they are being sent to do something to the opposition. Furthermore, they wear crowns of gold and have faces that resemble human ones and hair like that of women. These three images most likely suggest a reference to human authorities or royalty that are sources of evil beyond themselves, especially because the otherwise humanly pictured creatures have teeth like that of lions. The combination of elements is reminiscent of an Arab proverb that the locust has a horse's head, a lion's breast, a camel's feet, a serpent's body, and antennae like the hair of a woman. The picture is unnatural, diabolical—a terrifying picture of cruelty.

The lion's teeth, together with breastplates of iron and the sound of chariots and horses in battle, raise the spectre of ferocious warmaking. However, once again limits are put on their power—not only in the severity of their torture, but in its duration. Since the five months is actually the life cycle of the locust, the picture reminds us that evil has a limited life. As we shall see at the end of The Revelation, the God of truth and goodness will someday destroy it completely.

Finally, the description reveals the ultimate character of the locusts' king. He is called the angel of the abyss, and his names in Hebrew and Greek are Abaddon and Apollyon. These two names mean "Destruction" and "Destroyer," respectively, but for the early Christians to whom The Revelation was first written the latter name would have been much more specific. Indeed, the emperor Domitian (most likely the one persecuting the first readers of this book) claimed to be an incarnation of the Greek god Apollo.

In order to understand the next two woes, we need to see the overall framework in which we are working, which reinforces our interpretation of this section as one of grace. First, we were introduced to the three woes by the crying eagle (8:13), who warns the inhabitants of the earth about the woes to come. Then, since 9:12 specifically says that the first woe is past, we look for the completion of the other woes and are surprised to find that the second woe (which begins with the sounding of the sixth angel's trumpet in 9:13) ends with the resurrection of the two witnesses (11:11–14), who were trying to draw people back to Christ. Then, although the third woe is declared to be coming soon, no specific phrase in the book ever proclaims that it has ended. Instead, in the very next verses (15–19), with the sounding of the seventh angel's trumpet, the heavens break out in praise to God for his reign in justice. Those who are destroyed are those who have destroyed the earth.

Now when we return to the description of the second woe in chapter 9, we again notice many details of divine sovereignty. The voice comes directly from the golden altar that is before God (v. 13); the four angels are called to do their work (vv. 14–15); and God's control shows in the fact that they had been kept ready for this very task at "this very hour and day and month and year." They were to kill a third of humankind—and perhaps that symbolically divine number three throughout the sounding of the trumpets is also meant to indicate divine control over the amount of destruction. The troops are huge, numbering 200 million troops! Once again, their physical description is meant graphically to create an atmosphere. The breastplates of the riders were fiery red, dark blue, and yellow like sulfur, and out of the mouths of the horses came plagues of fire, smoke, and sulfur. Even the horses' tails, which were like snakes, inflicted injury—but why?

The key to this whole section comes in verses 20–21, which inform us that in spite of the two woes recorded in chapter 9 people were still too stubborn to turn back to God. The rest of humankind, those not killed by these plagues, still "did not repent of the works of their hands, so as not to worship demons, and the idols of gold and of silver and of brass and of stone and of wood, which can neither see nor hear nor walk." How ridiculous to worship such idols! Yet even the warning of the plagues had not sufficed to deter human beings from the vanity of their idol worship.

Revelation 9 ends with the very great tragedy that, in spite of all the different woes God has allowed throughout history (and with his longsuffering patience) in order to warn people, human beings have still willed to go their own way. They have not yet repented of all their earthly sins—symbolized by the list of four (murders, sorceries, immorality, and thefts).

Thus, the vision of the first six trumpets encourages all of us to spend time asking ourselves what trials God has allowed in order to call us back to himself. Of course, he does not inflict pain—the evil and brokenness of this world after the fall is its cause—but in his infinite care he knows that sometimes those loved must be allowed to experience discipline. Furthermore, when we turn to him repentantly, he reminds us again of the blood of the Lamb and the shepherding of his salvation (see Rev. 7:14–17 again).

Every time a new kind of physical affliction assails me I realize that many areas of my life are not yet in tune with God's best purposes. I do not submit willingly to reprimands, and sometimes in my bitterness or rebellion I stray further away and need an even more powerful reminder. (Sometimes it takes a two-by-four to get the mule back into the barn!) The greatest comfort to me in the trumpets of The Revelation is that God always sets limits. No locust or sulphur-mouthed horse can rage out of his control.

Although I can say the above about my own relationship with God, I may never judge others and say that their afflictions are meant by God to reprimand them and draw them back. The book of Job certainly teaches us that. His friends had no right to condemn him and blame his troubles on his sins. When God appeared, he didn't condemn Job, but instead pointed him to a foundation for the world other than the doctrine of retribution that both Job and his friends had espoused. Yet I know that I personally must join Job in the dust and ashes of repentance. When we have seen God, we all know that we are guilty.

The trumpets of Revelation 8–9 let us see God. His immense grace allows certain plagues to call human beings to repentance, but his sovereign control sets limits. His goal is to save.

22

Asking the Right Questions in Our Suffering: "How Long?" and "Meanwhile?"

Please refer often to Revelation 10:1–11:13 as you study this chapter.

Many times we deepen our own ethical dilemmas or are prevented from finding answers in them because we are asking the wrong questions. For example, single persons longing to marry often cause themselves problems in their relationships with the opposite sex because they ask the question, "Could it ever be right for me to marry this person?"—usually out of fear that they should break off the relationship to avoid causing themselves pain. Instead, they might ask positive questions about love in the Lord, questions such as "How can this particular friendship be a means for living out the principles of the kingdom of God?" or "How might this person and I be helpful to each other to deepen our relationship with the Lord and the effectiveness of our respective ministries?" Such questions would free single people to enjoy letting their friendships grow as God would have them grow, without an undue pressure toward marriage or toward the ungodliness of our society's sexual immorality.

Our church communities must more thoroughly teach skills of asking the right questions, of learning to think and discern, because our entertainment-oriented society fosters passive acceptance of its usually ungodly values. Christians especially need to ask critical questions—examining the patterns of our society to avoid becoming enculturated in values that do not follow the principles of Jesus; learning how to read the Scriptures in order to apply them appropriately to the issues of our times; and teaching our children to

153

search constantly for the ways of the kingdom of God in the midst of a corrupted and twisted world.

The urgency of asking the right questions is especially critical with such a project as reading The Revelation because we can so easily get bogged down in particulars and thereby miss the point that we should most essentially learn from the text. I am not saying that those particulars aren't important, nor that there aren't sometimes precise interpretations that aid us in understanding them, but their function must always be to point us more deeply to the message of the whole text. When we get so caught up in deciphering those particulars that the main thrust is missed, when we atomize the text, we lose the true, practical significance of the Word for our daily Christian lives.

In this chapter, therefore, we are going to practice focusing on the main questions that the text addresses and not worry too much about the many details of this section of The Revelation. The images of this portion from 10:1 to 11:13 are taken from numerous places in the First Testament, and digging them all out would prove very interesting for us, but I am confident that you can do that with the aid of a good cross-reference Bible.

Many of the images are quite precise. For example, the statement about the seven peals of thunder uttering their voices in 10:3 most likely refers to the seven occurrences of that phrase in Psalm 29 since the use of the particular article in "*the* seven thunders" seems to imply familiarity on the part of the readers. However, such details of specific scriptural references can be easily ferreted out if you are interested; I want instead to focus in this chapter on a larger picture.

The old outlining methods that we used in grade school can be very helpful for finding the larger patterns of a literary text. By outlining books of the Bible we can get an idea of the broad scope of a book's purposes and themes. If we were to outline the whole book of The Revelation together, we would have noticed by now a cyclical pattern that circulates throughout many places of the whole. The beginning of the book contains the circle of the seven letters to the seven churches, and now we have begun to see the cycles of the seven seals and the seven trumpets and the seven angels who blow those trumpets. A closer look at the patterns, however, reveals an interruption both between the sixth and the seventh seals (the two visions of Rev. 7) and then, when the trumpets follow the seals, the same kind of interlude between the sixth and the seventh trumpets. The two visions of 10:1–11:13 make up this interlude.

Both of these interruptions serve a literary purpose—in this case to focus on two significant questions: "How long?" and "What is the role of the people of God in the meanwhile?" We have seen and will continue to see that these two questions form the backbone of The Revelation. God teaches the saints that their first question is not answered in terms of how long the suffering must yet go on, but with God's reversal of this question to them: "How long will it be till the church goes about its duty in the meanwhile?" Furthermore, the duty of the church in the meanwhile is revealed as this: "To witness to the sovereignty of God that seems to be hidden in this meanwhile." These are still the primary issues for God's people today. This is the challenge for each of us personally: how can my life manifest God's lordship?

For several years my daily meditation focused on the Psalms,[1] and in this project I was repeatedly encouraged to become more theocentrically focused, to turn around that question "How long?" in order to ask instead, "Who is God in the midst of this?" This is the lesson of true biblical patience that we have been learning here in The Revelation, too. Such patience does not mean waiting until things change, but learning to wait because of who God is even when things don't change. Such a change of focus, instead, enables us to ask a different question and to search for a different answer.

The structure of Revelation 10 seems to underscore the appropriateness of such an approach to this section, because at first we are told of a message from the thunders that the seer was not allowed to reveal. Immediately thereafter, however, the angel does make it plain that there will be no more delay.

We simply cannot understand all the mysteries of God. Certain things cannot be revealed to us, perhaps because we can't handle them; but this message is unquestionable: there is no more delay. God's purposes must be accomplished now.

The aura of mystery that surrounds this text is wonderfully captured by the composer Olivier Messiaen in his quartet *Quatuor pour la fin du temps* ("Quartet for the End of Time"), inspired by this text,

155

for violin, cello, clarinet, and piano. This piece first captured my interest because of its title; then a stunning performance (in connection with the Anne Frank exhibit) of its graphic music and the composer's own biblical and mystical comments led me to new questions and a renewed theocentric focus. Written while he was imprisoned by the Nazis in 1941, Messiaen's *Quartet* includes these movements:

1. Crystalline Liturgy
2. Vocalise for the Angel Who Announces the End of Time
3. The Abyss of the Birds
4. Interlude
5. Praise to the Eternity of Jesus
6. Dance of Fury for the Seven Trumpets
7. Tangles of Rainbows for the Angel Who Announces the End of Time
8. Praise to the Immortality of Jesus

Especially in the fifth movement, in which a broad cello melody "magnifies with love and reverence the eternity of the powerful and sweet Word,"[2] this mysterious music captures not only the rainbow colors of the angel, but also some of the "moments of silent adoration and marvelous visions of peace" of The Revelation. Messiaen himself and three other inmates first performed the quartet on damaged instruments in the prison camp at Görlitz in Silesia— but in the midst of it all Messiaen was able to rest in the mystery of Christ's sovereignty and offer his music as a witness to "the harmonies of heaven."

That is an incredibly important message for the Christian community in our times. We might not have all the answers, but because of those that we do have, we must certainly get on with our task of manifesting to the world the undeniable reality of the sovereign lordship of Christ. Even in our imprisonments we can make music!

Think of all the questions about which we are confused. It might not be time yet for us to know the final answers. My favorite assurance is the passage in Habakkuk that reminds us that the vision awaits its time (Hab. 2:1–4). It will not delay, nor will it be too late. If it tarries, we are to learn to wait for it. At the right time God's purposes will be accomplished, even as they were for Israel. Meanwhile, "the just shall live by faith."

When we don't know the answers to all of life's questions, we can ask different ones—questions of how we can best be stewards of this time in the meanwhile. How can we fulfill the purposes of the kingdom with the information that we do have? That makes our approach to life so much easier. In the example that began this chapter, single people can learn how to deal with relationships. They can look in friendships for how God's purposes can best be accomplished at the moment without knowing what might become of them in the future. The immense pressures toward marriage or for sex put on friendships by our surrounding culture spoil many relationships. Our Christian communities could be a means of support for persons establishing deep relationships in the love of Christ without the added burdens of our culture's pressures.[3]

This is another lesson I learned from my friends Tim and Linden. Years ago I grew to love both men more deeply than I could have ever imagined—and I know they love me that way, too—without romance, though with godly affection, and thoroughly in a growing *agape* love that will continue to keep us friends throughout life and on into heaven. Though I was alone and lonely at the time, I truly rejoiced when they both found lovely wives—and then they both wrote celebrative letters to me when I became engaged. Asking the right kind of questions freed us thoroughly to enjoy each other's gifts to us when we were all single without spoiling the relationships by romantic games or sexual exploitation.

In Revelation 10:9 the seer is instructed to eat the scroll and to find it both sweet and bitter, much in the manner of the prophet Ezekiel (chapters 2 and 3). Then he is commanded to speak the message of God to all the peoples, nations, tongues, and kings. Once again a fourfold typology reminds us that every aspect of earthly existence must be touched by the prophetic message. Furthermore, the inclusion of kings this time emphasizes that the Word of God must be spoken especially in the high places. God's Word of prophetic judgment and of hope has a place in the halls of government and in the hearts of rulers. However, we must always remember that it is a prophetic word. God does not call the church to take over government; never dare it force its control on others, though perhaps Christians might serve in political capacities and certainly must with great integrity speak a careful prophetic word.

Speaking the Word is the church's task. The answer to our first question, "How long?" is that there can be no delay. God's people must be faithful now to proclaim his message. Furthermore, the answer to the question of the community's task is to speak truly the Word God gives us to proclaim. That is why the second of the two intervening visions introduces the image of the two witnesses.

Countless interpretations have been offered for the vision of the two witnesses in Revelation 11. Scholars debate whether the picture should be taken literally, or whether the temple symbolically represents the people of God, so that measuring its inner courts stresses the protection and security God gives to his people. Do the outer courts that are not to be measured represent the part of the church that has compromised with the world? Is the fate of the witnessing church the message from the scroll that could not be revealed? How do these visions relate to each other?

And who are the two witnesses? Different commentators suggest various theories: Israel and the New Testament church; the Law and the Prophets; the Law and the Gospel; the Old/First and the New/Second Testaments; Zerubbabel and Joshua; Elijah and Elisha; James and John; Peter and Paul; the churches of Smyrna and Philadelphia (which, of all the seven, were not called to repentance); Moses and Elijah; and so forth. The latter pair seems especially likely because of the references to the plagues and the turning of water into blood (Moses: Ex. 9:14; 7:14–18) and to the holding up of the rain for 3½ years and consuming enemies with fire (Elijah: 1 Kings 17:1; 2 Kings 1:10–12). Moreover, these two figures had talked with Jesus on the Mount of Transfiguration, and both had ended their earthly lives in unusual ways—with Moses being buried by God himself (Deut. 34:6) and Elijah ascending in the fiery chariot (2 Kings 2:11).

Even if we could know absolutely that the two witnesses of 11:1–13 were Moses and Elijah, still we would have to ask other, larger questions: Why do they appear at this place in The Revelation? What is their message to us?

Again, we have to see the two witnesses as part of the larger literary whole of the entire Revelation, and once again our key lies in overviewing an important element of the overall pattern. In 11:2–3 the numbers 42 (months) and 1,260 (days) are used—the first number with the negative event of the trampling of the holy city, and the second number with the positive work of the two witnesses, who proclaimed God's message during the same length of time.

These two numbers also occur in chapters 12 and 13 in connection with the story of the pregnant woman and the dragon, and once again 1,260 is used there positively, to describe the fact that the woman was protected by God in a place he prepared for her (12:6). The number of 42 months (13:5) is used again negatively to tell us that the beast was given a mouth to utter blasphemies and to exercise his authority for that length of time. Furthermore, this later section also uses a third figure (in 12:14) to represent the same amount of time ("time, times and half a time," which probably means one year, plus two years, plus ½ a year) in connection with the woman's being cared for by God in his sovereignty.

These three figures (1,260 days, 42 months, and 3½ years), equaling the same amount of time, seem to tell us that three different things are happening at once. When we look carefully, we discover that they correspond to the three ideas composing the underlying structure of the entire Revelation: Even though satanic opposition continues for a time, God is sovereign Lord and provides for us and protects us during that time; therefore, the saints can continue faithfully to endure those meanwhiles.

When we apply this basic underlying structure to the story of the two witnesses, we can see some important lessons. Yes, they are besieged by the enemy, who tramples on the holy city for 42 months. In fact, they are killed by that enemy. Yet they are faithful in carrying out their task for those same 1,260 days. They are patient for the meanwhile and respond to the "how long?" questions with faithfulness to their tasks. Therefore, though they are killed, they are restored by the sovereignty of their Lord.

Since the number of 3½ years likely suggested to the original readers of The Revelation the significance of "time, times and half a time" in Daniel 7:25 and then in the history of the people of Israel, all of this becomes even more poignant. From 167 to 164 B.C., the outrageous emperor Antiochus Epiphanes IV had desecrated the temple and reviled the God of the Jews in his vicious campaigns against them. However, after 3½ years the uprisings led by the Maccabee family finally restored some measure of Israelite dignity, and the temple was reconsecrated for its service.

These memories would have made this message of The Revelation clear to its readers in the first century: the ravishings of the present emperor might be severe (as a manifestation of the demonic opposition that characterizes world history), but Christ (the Son of Man in Daniel 7) is still the sovereign Lord, and so we can be faithful to his purposes, knowing that eventually he will vindicate his people and restore his temple. (In fact, as we shall see at the end of The Revelation, there will no longer be a need for the temple, for the presence of the Lord himself will be all his people need.)

The message for the 20th century is the same: God's ultimate sovereignty empowers our faithfulness. As various empires desecrate our places of worship or mock our faith, we can respond with diligent witnessing, knowing that the sovereign Lord will eventually triumph and vindicate his people.

What is the witnessing task of the church today? We proclaim the sovereignty of God, not of the nations. Perhaps that might take the form of speaking against the pretensions of nations that would seek to control the world by means of a nuclear arsenal large enough to demolish everything. Perhaps our task is to proclaim to kings the judgment—and hope—of God. Most of all, our task is to live faithfully the ethics of God's kingdom in our own communities, to stand as a witnessing people against the lifestyle of a world that wears the mark of the beast on its forehead and right hand (see the following chapter). We are to be a people marked instead with the Father's name, persons who live in total dependence on him. And then, even if we are killed in the process of such a witness, we will be called to come up to heaven, and the world will be astonished at the greatness of the sovereign God (Rev. 11:12–13).

Notes

1. This study led to my book *I'm Lonely, LORD—How Long?* (San Francisco: Harper and Row, 1983).

2. These quotations are Messiaen's own words, translated by Helen Baker for the Musical Heritage Society's recording of the *Quatuor pour la fin du temps*.

3. See my book on this subject, *Sexual Character: Beyond Technique to Intimacy* (Eerdmans, 1993).

23

42 Months, 1,260 Days, and 3½ Years

Please refer often to Revelation 11:14–12:17 as you study this chapter.

In my childhood, advertisements for one brand of toothpaste showed an visible plastic shield standing around a great big tooth being bombarded by projectiles of decay and plaque. Somehow that image has stuck with me all these years as a singularly appropriate picture of the spiritual life.

We are like teeth, highly susceptible to all kinds of spiritual injury and decay. Just because we have become Christians does not mean we won't encounter opposition. However, God has put up a shield around us—invisible to the rest of the world, but durable and impenetrable. Nothing can get through that shield as long as we remain enclosed in it. Of course, we often step outside of it. Nevertheless, the shield is always there.

The three key messages of The Revelation are again clear in its 12th chapter. However, this section adds some essential insights to prepare us for the major depiction of the forces of evil in chapters 13 and 14.

We are prepared for something very important by the immediate introduction to the major picture of this section. After the announcement that the third woe is coming and the sounding of the seventh angel's trumpet (11:14–15), loud voices remind us that Christ is Lord and that he will reign forever and ever. The elders worship God because his reign is beginning; the nations are going to be judged and the saints rewarded. Meanwhile, the temple in heaven is opened, the ark is revealed (to remind us of God's covenant faithfulness), and the usual signs of God's theophany (lightning, rumblings, thunder, earthquake, and hailstorm) occur.

However, these events are all a prelude to the picture of the woman in chapter 12.

The seer proclaims that a great sign appeared in heaven (12:1). In both The Revelation and John's gospel, the word *sign* carries important connotations. Choosing that word instead of *miracles* (as used by the other three gospel writers), the evangelist John in his gospel emphasizes with the seven (symbolizing "perfect") signs that Jesus is divine. Signs should be accepted as true in themselves—i.e., the miracles really did happen—but they are of secondary importance. Most essentially, we notice to whom the signs point.

Think, for example, of a sign to the beach. The sign is important; it helps us find the beach. However, we wouldn't park our car at it and enjoy only the sign. The sign is true, but of secondary importance. This understanding is essential for reading the fantastic accounts of The Revelation: The signs point to something beyond themselves, to which we should pay primary attention.

Our attention in this chapter should primarily be focused on the two major opponents: Satan and Christ. They are both clearly named in verses 9 and 10, which serve as the focus of Revelation 12.

The major power of evil is named both with all his titles (the great dragon, the serpent of old, the devil, and Satan) and with the description that he deceives the whole world and was thrown down to the earth with all his angels. Christ, on the other hand, is named by showing that the forces of evil cannot have their way at all. A loud voice in heaven proclaims that the salvation, power, and kingdom of God, as well as the authority that God has invested in Christ, have all come and that the accuser has been thrown down. Consequently, the saints can overcome him by the blood of the Lamb.

The vignette preceding this climax also names Christ, by showing that God's methods for overcoming the forces of evil were highly unorthodox: God accomplished his purpose by sending a child.

The description of the woman in 12:1–2 is simple, in great contrast to the picture of the harlot in 17:3–6. Clothed with the sun and moon and stars, she carries all the light. The number of 12 stars reminds us of the children of God, his people. She is very pregnant, crying to give birth.

We should not try to pin down too tightly the identity of this woman. Many have thought that she symbolizes Mary because of the description of her child, but she certainly represents more than Mary, for this is not a picture of Christ's birth in historical time. A more likely identity would be Eve, who is the bearer of all humanity, as well as of the promised Seed. We will notice other details that expand the symbolism as we work through the text.

The powers of evil are introduced next, the beginning of a parody that is thoroughly sketched in chapters 13 and 14. The dragon imitates God the Father, having the perfect number (7) of heads and diadems and the complete number (10) of horns (a symbol throughout the Scriptures of power).

The fact that we should not take any of these images in The Revelation literalistically is indicated by the account of the dragon disrupting a third of the stars of heaven with his tail (12:4). In 6:13 all the stars had already fallen out of the sky, and in 8:12 a third of them were destroyed again. (Remember The Revelation's use of restatement and cyclical development of basic themes.) The image here can emphasize that the dragon caused a lot of disturbance and that his efforts resulted in people losing the light. The main point, however, is that the dragon awaited the birth of the child so that he could devour him (v. 4). However, to do so was an impossible notion on the part of the dragon (v. 5), because the child was to rule all the nations with a rod of iron, and he was protected by God himself and caught up to his throne.

This child's rescue leads to two significant events: the woman flees and the dragon is angry. We saw in my previous chapter that different numbers are used in The Revelation to indicate the same amount of time and several concurrent themes. This second use of the 1,260 days (v. 6) indicates that throughout Satan's harassment God's people can know that his protection is secure. God himself had prepared the place for the woman, and she was not merely kept there. Rather, she was thoroughly nourished during that time.

Meanwhile, the dragon waged war with Michael and the angels. Of course, the powers of evil (which are not strong enough) can never defeat the powers of good, and there is no place for the evil ones in heaven (since they choose to contradict God's purposes); so they were cast out (12:7–9).

Notice how "untimed" this whole account is. Some associate the story of the woman of verses 1–2 with Mary (mothering Jesus), but this war in heaven (vv. 7–9) is usually considered to have taken place before the foundation of the world or at least at the beginning of time. Furthermore, verse 11 describes the saints who overcame the powers of evil and records their victory in a past tense, which carries us into the years after the resurrection of Christ. Obviously, we can't take its images literalistically and put them on a calendar, for they are meant to be understood in an eternal (i.e., a timeless) framework. These images show the continued conflict of the forces of good and evil—all the way from the beginning with Eve (perhaps an implication of the sudden shift to the word *serpent* in 12:14–15)—although the end of The Revelation will clearly demonstrate that the powers of good will ultimately triumph.

Satan was thrown out of heaven, yet he accuses the brothers and sisters before God day and night (12:10). However, this Satan can be overcome. The most significant aspect of the entire story in Revelation 12 is that he is overcome by the blood of the Lamb and by the word of the saints' testimony and by their willingness even to die. It would require a separate book on the concept of the principalities and powers to explicate thoroughly the exact biblical description of Christ's conquest of the powers at the cross and the implications of that victory for our daily encounters with the powers of evil,[1] but we can notice at this point that the saints are able to overcome because the Lamb's blood has been shed.

Furthermore, the saints overcome evil by their testimony (which links us to the work of the two witnesses in the previous chapter) and by not loving their lives even to death (v. 11). By this reference to their willingness to suffer for the sake of the kingdom of God, John encouraged his original readers as they faced the persecutions of the emperor.

Similarly, as God's people today struggle with various physical or spiritual setbacks or challenges, we can also be greatly comforted that our sufferings are part of overcoming the powers of evil. Sometimes in our personal trials we think that we are being overcome by the powers of evil instead, but this text offers us genuine hope. Though we undergo sufferings, these, too, can be the means for

God's purposes to be accomplished. Consequently, we can join the heavens and all who dwell there in their rejoicing (12:12).

However, we must also pay attention to the call of woe given to the earth and sea. Indeed, our earth and sea have suffered tremendously because of the wrath of the evil powers. We might think of such things as pollution of the rivers and oceans, acid rain, the damage to the ozone layer, etc. These are some of the contemporary visible signs of the cosmic warfare. True, we realize that these are effects of human greed and consumption, but the prince of evil's major way of working is through the disruption of God's purposes for people, so that people themselves become agents of his destruction. The original readers of The Revelation would have seen the suffering of the earth, for example, in the war tactics of various empires, in contrast to God's specific commands to his people to care for the earth—such as the instruction not to harm the fruit-bearing trees in wars (Deut. 20:19) or to let the fields lie fallow every seven years (Lev. 25:3–5). The powers of evil want to undo God's good creation; the cosmic warfare has earthly consequences.

That is why the Christian community must be concerned about such things as ecological destruction, to do as much as we can to avoid contributing to it ourselves, and to challenge others to change their habits. As one tiny example, our congregation stopped using Styrofoam cups during our fellowship hours, since those cups contribute immensely to the pollution of the earth. (With one restaurant chain in the United States each year adding 1.5 billion cubic feet of Styrofoam waste to our earth's destruction, how much might congregational fellowship hours throughout the land contribute to the load?) We hung up huge mug racks to hold each member's personal mug and several extras for visitors. More important, the mugs symbolize and force us to ask deeper questions about how the principalities and powers vent their wrath in our world, especially by playing on our greed. Our little habits of carefulness make us more aware of the larger issues at stake in the cosmic battle for all of God's creation and the souls of human beings.

The devil has great wrath because he knows that he has only a short time (12:12). Certainly we have seen the effects of that in our present society. It seems sometimes that everything is getting so much worse so much faster. Just as a losing ball team scrambles desperately in the last minutes of a game to try to overcome the deficit in points, so the powers of evil are working at full blast because they know their days are numbered.

The dragon especially wants to get rid of the woman who produced the male child. The scenario is almost like a James Bond movie—only better because the woman never resorts to any violence or trickery or sexual immorality. No matter what the dragon comes up with to try to destroy her, God creates some sort of rescue. First (v. 14), on the wings of a great eagle she flies to the place that, we remember, God had prepared to nourish her (v. 6). The image of the eagle is used throughout the First Testament to describe the continual care of God for his people, so this figure in The Revelation must have been extremely comforting to its readers. Verse 14 also specifically states that she was nourished for time, times and half a time—the 3½ years that corresponds to the 1,260 days and reinforces our conclusion (see the previous chapter) that, even though the powers of evil rage for 42 months (the same amount of time), they can't overcome the power of God.

The serpent (this great deluder changes his form constantly) then spews out a river of water from his mouth to try to sweep her away with the flood (v. 15), but this time the earth comes to her rescue and swallows it up. This picture reminds us that God intervened at the time of Noah so that all humanity would not be destroyed.

Finally (v. 17), the dragon gave up his attempts to destroy the woman when he saw the way she was protected, so he turned his attention to the rest of her offspring (a statement that again causes us to resist the temptation to identify her solely with Mary). Almost as if to mark the end of this scene with a flourish, the seer describes her offspring more specifically as the ones who keep God's commandments and hold to the testimony of Jesus. In other words, Satan has turned his attention to all of us believers because he could not conquer the child or its mother or Michael and his angels.

Thus, he continues to make war. While the whole parody will be described more thoroughly in the next chapter, we clearly note here that the dragon cannot get us. God's love and grace will always protect us as we "obey God's commandments and hold to the testimony of Jesus"—by wings of eagles, by the earth and God's creation, and, most of all, by the blood of the Lamb and the Word.

Note

1. See Marva J. Dawn, "The Concept of 'The Principalities and Powers' in the Works of Jacques Ellul" (University of Notre Dame: Ph.D. dissertation, 1992).

24

Taking the Presence of Evil Seriously

Please refer often to Revelation 13–14 as you study this chapter.

One morning during a stay in Wisconsin I enjoyed "Breakfast on the Farm" to help celebrate "June Is Dairy Month." I found it very interesting to listen to folks compare the calories, protein value, nutrition, and other qualities of various dairy products with those of their imitation substitutes. However, I still can't taste the difference between butter and margarine. I guess one has to be educated to know the difference—or else be born a true Wisconsinite.

Spiritually, we have to be born a Christian through the Holy Spirit *and* be educated into the values of the kingdom of God to know the difference between what is true and what is a corrupted imitation. First, God brings us into relationship with himself, and his love and grace free us from the control of sin that causes us to choose imitations. Then, the Spirit forms us through the Word, used by the Christian community, to "have the mind of Christ." Apart from this grace lie the destruction and despair of devilish deceptions.

For example, the problem with a sexual relationship before marriage is that it actually produces the opposite of what the individual is truly seeking. Those who turn to sex in order to belong or to find the protection and loving care that create security find instead that outside of a permanent covenant of commitment a sexual relationship leads to greater insecurity. They never know if they are really loved as persons or if only their bodies are lustfully desired. A momentary commitment without commitment destroys trust. On the other hand, those who turn to sex for its immediate pleasure eventually experience that, ripped out of its rightful context, sex without meaning is not thoroughly satisfying.

That is the case with all of the devil's corruptions. The powers of evil take what was originally good in God's design and twist it into the opposite. Leadership dominance often leads to downfall; hoarding of money leads to greater fears of losing it; possession of great luxury only aggravates the desire for more; achieving the place of number one leads to greater pressure to stay there. Our society's overabundance of heart disease, high blood pressure, and other tension-related diseases points to the corruption of that which was originally created good.

You know that quite well already. What we don't as readily recognize is the very perversion of the powers of evil themselves.

The secret to cracking the code of Revelation 12 and 13 is to recognize its devilish parody. The dragon and the beasts represent the powers of evil in their corrupted imitation of the real power of God, and the three characters who dominate the scene parody in turn the Father, Son, and Holy Spirit of the Trinity. Notice the following, striking correspondences in the text:

The dragon (comparable to the Father) has the perfect number (7) of heads (for wisdom) and crowns (for dignity and authority) and a complete number (10) of horns (for power). Rev. 12:3

The dragon fought with God for his place and was hurled out of heaven as a result. Rev. 12:7–9

The first beast (who parodies Christ) similarly has 7 heads and 10 horns (even as Christ has perfect likeness to the Father). Rev. 13:1

Like God the Father, the dragon gave his power and throne and great authority to the beast (the Son). This grouping of three (the divine number) underscores the way that these parody God's true power and throne and authority. Rev. 13:2

The beast had suffered a fatal wound, but had been healed (or "resurrected" like Christ). Rev. 13:3

The whole world was astonished by this and followed after the beast (just as the crowds followed Jesus). Rev. 13:3

Human beings worshiped the dragon because he had given authority to the beast (even as people worshiped God the Father because of the Son, which Jesus declared to be his purpose.) Rev. 13:4

The phrase "Who is like the beast and who can make war against him?" parodies Exodus 15:11 and its question about God. Rev. 13:4

The beast was given power and authority for 42 months (approximately the amount of time in the public ministry of Jesus, though this number could also symbolize the reign of Antiochus Epiphanes IV as described in chapter 23 above). Rev. 13:5

The beast was given authority over every tribe, people, language, and nation (the four classes representing the whole earth). Even as in Daniel 7:13–14 such authority was given to the Son of Man, so The Revelation has stressed repeatedly that the sovereignty over all the four corners of the earth belongs to the reign of the Christ. Rev. 13:7

All those whose names are not written in the book of the Lamb will worship the beast, even as Jesus told his disciples that one is either for him or against him. Rev. 13:8

The second beast (comparable to the Holy Spirit) exercises the authority of the first beast on his behalf, just as Jesus said the Holy Spirit would come in his place and be like him (see John 16:13–14). Rev. 13:12

Just as the Holy Spirit works, the second beast caused the earth to worship the first beast, whose fatal wound had been healed. Rev. 13:12

Just like the Holy Spirit, the second beast performed great miracles and signs that would cause the people of the earth to believe in the first beast (the Son). Rev. 13:13–14

The fact that the second beast can cause the sign of fire to come down in the presence of others reminds us of the Pentecost event. Rev. 13:13

The most gruesome of all the parodies is the fact that the second beast gives a mark to all the inhabitants of the earth who follow him. Ephesians 1:13–14 talks about Christians being marked with the Holy Spirit and sealed by him for their spiritual inheritance, and Revelation 7:3 spoke of the sealing of the believers (see also Gal. 6:17). Rev. 13:16

The mark of this second beast is given on either the right hand or the forehead. In Jewish thought, hands represent one's deeds—as in the phrase "He who has clean hands and a pure heart" (Ps. 24:4), which signifies someone who is clean both outside and inside (in his actions/outward behavior and in his thoughts/will). Furthermore, the right hand is the symbol for fellowship in Semitic cultures, so a mark on it represents that with which the individual is associated and the actions of one's lifestyle.

To be marked on one's forehead represents one's thinking. That is why on their foreheads and hands the Jewish people wore *tephillin* (plural of the Hebrew noun that means "prayer")—small, square black cases containing passages from the Torah. These little boxes reminded them to conform their thinking and their behavior to the plan and purposes of God. Even so, the parody of the beast stresses that those who belong to him become like him, recognizing his authority over their thinking and deeds.

The beast's number, 666, has probably raised more speculation than any other symbolic number in the Scriptures. Various people have given me numerous reports about certain documents coming out from computers and Social Security checks bearing this beastly number. Frequently people have declared to me that a great computer in Belgium, with all the vital data about all of us, is being used in an attempt to take over the world—and that scares many seriously devoted Christians who see in its operations the work of the beast.

Unfortunately, such fears cause us to miss the fact that the mark of the beast is already displayed all over our world and has been ever since The Revelation was written.

Biblical numerologists report that in the Jewish system of numbering the letters in the Hebrew alphabet, the number 666 is equal to the sum of the letters used in spelling the name of Nero, whose persecution of Christians had been especially gruesome. Therefore, even if The Revelation was written later, during the reign of Domitian, that earlier emperor represented by this code number 666 would stand for all the persecutions by the Roman state.

A larger explanation, however, teaches us more. Repeatedly in The Revelation, as we have seen, the number 7 symbolizes perfection, and 3 stands for divinity or godliness/spirituality. In contrast, in

Hebrew thought the number 6 signifies what is less than perfect and, therefore, that which is corrupted or evil. The number 6 is the number of fallibility, less than the perfect 7. To put three 6s together, then, is to divinize that which is not divine, to make sacred what is marred or imperfect. Thus, anything in our thoughts or lifestyle that elevates to the position of a god things that are merely human or actually evil is marked as the work of the beast. The number 666 symbolizes all our allegiances to the gods of this world.

When I first began teaching about the book of Revelation, the Washington state lottery had just been instituted to try to solve the state's financial problems. Initially, I was distressed that many Christians were so excited about the chance to win the lottery, which seemed to me to violate biblical principles of earning one's own bread and of stewardship, and I began to see in that system the mark of the beast. Over the years I have seen again and again the subtle and corrupting power of various forms of gambling, the deceptive ways that Mammon becomes a god.

As part of my doctoral work in ethics, I was stunned to learn from economists all the deleterious effects of lottery systems. They become a regressive tax system because participants tend primarily to come from lower classes, those who try desperately to win under the illusion that they can solve all their financial problems forever with just a little luck—the chances of which are terribly slim. Moreover, such systems decrease the normal, taxable revenues of stores, because folks are investing in lottery tickets instead of regular commodities. General income is thus diverted from useful products. Furthermore, if the proceeds from the lottery are used to finance such things as education, often voters will reject the kind of steady tax support that schools need. What bothers me most, however, is that the system merely coats over the real source of a state's financial problems rather than digging to the heart of the matter: assessing the inefficacies of state management and correcting them from the inside.

The lottery is just one contemporary example of many (such as the Savings and Loan scandal) that we could choose to demonstrate the power of Mammon and the mark of the beast. Jesus warned his disciples extensively about the power of this god. These chapters in The Revelation stir us Christians, who can face life realistically because we know the source of genuine hope, to be on the cutting edge warning the world about the demonic deceptions that we see. If we speak as prophets, we will not necessarily be heard, but it is our Christian duty at least to speak. As God commanded Ezekiel, so we must warn the people. If they fail to listen, then we are not responsible. However, we are responsible if we haven't warned them. (See Ezek. 2 and 3, especially 3:18–19.)

What other elements of our society illustrate the mark of the beast? When our youth think certain brands of clothing are absolutely essential so that they make an idolatry out of wearing them, is the mark of the beast on their right hands? When the success syndrome, the I-don't-care-whom-I-kill-just-so-I'm-number-one attitude that dominates our culture, invades our thinking, have we marked our foreheads with a 666?

Tragically, the mark of the beast can be evident also in our churches. Sometimes congregations attract kids to Bible school by offering prizes of trips or bicycles, so that the motivation is to win the world's possessions and not because the love of Jesus possesses us. Too easily parishes thrive on the world's images of success—vast numbers or immense parish facilities—rather than in the deepening of genuine discipleship. These divinizations of human goals demonstrate that the powers of evil are dominating the thought and actions.

In contrast to the great parody of the dragon and the two beasts in chapters 12 and 13, Revelation 14 immediately describes the Lamb standing with the 144,000 who have been marked instead with the name of God and who are singing new songs. This number, like 666, is also symbolic and represents the whole people of God by means of 12 (the tribes of Israel) times 12 (the new covenant people) times 10 (the number of completeness) multiplied by itself 3 (the divine number) times.

In all the tension and anxiety over the 666s coming out of computers, many Christians don't realize that the mark of the beast is constantly displayed in our world. Similarly, we need to be reminded that these next verses in chapter 14 are also continuously being fulfilled. Indeed, the people of God bear on their minds and countenances the radiance of their relationship with God. Every time a Christian composer writes a new song or excited Christians burst out with a new hymn of praise, they join the 144,000 in their songs before the throne.

We do not have to be afraid of how this imagery of the mark of the beast might be fulfilled some day by the world takeover of a giant computer. Rather, we should be afraid of how that imagery is being constantly fulfilled whenever we divinize human things in our lives, whenever we let that which might have been good become corrupted and beastly/demonic.

How do things become gods to us? Are we tyrannized by power, prestige, popularity, television, hobbies, music of any sort (classical music becomes a snare to me when it becomes more important than listening to someone who needs my care), clothes (whether luxurious or offbeat), or possessions of any sort (like books, gardens, computers, homes, and so forth)? All these things parody the abundant life that Jesus promised us, a life available to us only when our thinking and lifestyle reflect the relationship we have with God—desiring his values, seeking his kingdom, living out his purposes. All else is blasphemy and a parody of his will.

We in the church can learn from each other how to "follow the Lamb wherever he goes" (14:4). The elderly, out of their many years of experience, or the physically challenged, who are denied many of the opportunities that able-bodied people routinely have, can perhaps discuss with us what they have learned about the illusions of the beast's mark. My wheelchair-bound friend Linden once told me how he had come clearly to see that he would never be able to build the kind of lifestyle many in our culture crave, because so much of his financial resources had to be used to hire aides for his personal care. He was grateful that the lures of owning a sailboat, enjoying various sports, or participating in many of the activities of the night life did not appeal to him at all because these possible idolatries were inherently inaccessible to him. Because circumstances limit him to the simple things that sustain life, he is more aware of the Joy of that simplicity than those of us capable of attaining more pretentious lifestyles. Similarly, persons with terminal illness often report how imminent death forces them to learn the true value of things. Diagnosed with cancer, I too feel a heightened urgency to concentrate on what is truly important.

Again, those who have little are usually much more willing to share than those who hoard their vast possessions. Statistics show that the poor give a much larger proportion of their income to caring for others. This was also demonstrated to me powerfully by some of the poor people who cared for me when I recently taught in Mexico. Those who have little know that the true value of things is multiplied by sharing.

The idolatries of our culture, symbolized by the mark of the beast, beckon us with illusions of wealth, power, position, and success. In contrast, the Father's love in Christ frees us from the control of these and other gods. Jesus offers us an alternative model of giving, submission, humility, and even suffering for the sake of the kingdom, and the Holy Spirit empowers us to live in those ways that stand against the mark of the beast. In our limitations we learn the Joy of total dependence on the triune God, whose mark of ownership is on our foreheads.

25

We Wouldn't Want Love without Holiness

Please refer often to Revelation 15–16 as you study this chapter.

I remember a time in elementary school when I was given a lower grade than another student even though I had done better work. Even at that young age I knew it was unjust and questioned the unfair punishment. In contrast, a doctoral professor whom I continue to respect greatly once gave me a B even though I had worked extremely hard and had done more than many of the other students. I didn't question that grade, however, because I recognized my deficiencies and aimed to correct them in the next semester. The professor's assessment was just.

On a much larger scale, many question the justice of God. The text from The Revelation that lies before us in these chapters makes it clear that, even when God vents his wrath, God's judgments are always both just and loving.

We are warned by the opening sentence of this scene that we are about to encounter a very important event. The seer tells us that he saw another sign in heaven, great and marvelous, and that the seven plagues the seven angels held were the last because in them the wrath of God is finished (15:1).

Before we see that final venting of God's wrath, however, we hear a song of praise to God for his justice. The exaltation of the song is heightened by the preceding description of those who sang it. All of them have come away victorious from the work of the beast, from his image, and from the number of his name. Furthermore, they stand on a sea of glass that seems to be mixed with fire. Finally, even the harps they hold are given to them by God. Every element in this description heightens our awareness that these saints truly are God's people, committed to him and faithful in his service.

Moreover, the songs they sing are those of Moses, God's faithful bondservant, and of the Lamb. Perhaps these titles are meant to indicate the whole counsel of God, since Moses certainly represents the First Testament as the Lamb represents the Second. Certainly the song that follows is composed of bits and snatches from many portions of the Scriptures, both Hebrew and Greek. We won't trace all of those connections here (since you can readily find them yourself in any good commentary or cross-reference Bible). Rather, the important note for our purposes is that the song exalts the righteousness, the truth, the justice of God's ways. That is certainly the reminder that we need before we encounter the scene of God's final wrath.

We have to hear this content of the song especially because people in our culture often object that they can't believe in a God who punishes people. "I believe in a God who loves everybody," they say. "Certainly you can't believe that there is a hell. If God is really loving, then doesn't he want to save everyone?" Such comments demonstrate the common problem of reducing the complexity of God's dialectical character to a single attribute. If we see God only as loving, we will forget that he is also just and holy. If we concentrate only on his justice, we might lose his grace by overemphasizing his wrath.

God is both loving and holy. Certainly his love pervades his justice (as we shall see in the following pictures of his wrath), but his justice must be weighed nonetheless, or else ultimately everything would be unfair. Even my childhood insight prevented me from accepting unfairness. Those who want only a loving God would reject that one-sidedness, too, if they seriously considered its implications.

Instead, the song of the angels recognizes that when the nations genuinely see the righteousness and truth of God's ways, they will come to worship the Lord, who is indeed King of the nations (15:3–4). This song gives us a model for dealing with those who want only a loving God. When we listen to people who decry God's wrath, we do not need to defend his ways. Rather, we want to show them how the righteousness of his ways has already been revealed.

In 15:5–8 the descriptions of the angels who undertake the task remind us again of the holiness and purity of God in his actions of wrath. First, we are told that they came out of the temple of the tabernacle of testimony in heaven (a pictorial stacking that underscores the holiness of their origin). Next, their image is one of clean, bright, pure linen and golden sashes. Finally, the bowls they are given are golden.

Most important is that the angels' description is undergirded with the themes of the character of God. The angels deliver the wrath of the one who lives forever and ever, the one whose glory and power fill the temple with smoke (a reminder of the scene in Isaiah 6, to which the prophet responded with a sense of his uncleanness because he had seen the holy God).

The same theme of the righteousness and justice of God's acts is carried into the description in chapter 16 of the first three plagues and the response they elicited. Verse 2 insists that when the bowl of the plague was poured out on the earth it became a loathsome and malignant sore *only* on the ones who had the mark of the beast and had worshiped his image. In addition, in response to the second and third plagues, both the angel of the waters and the altar raise another hymn of praise to God for the righteousness of his judgments (16:5–7). Moreover, those plagues resemble the blood plague in Egypt and would have, no doubt, reminded the initial readers of The Revelation of the righteous significance of God's intervention there in the Israelites' lives.

With the pouring of the fourth bowl the theme of repentance is introduced. The responses to both the fourth and fifth plagues (vv. 9 and 11) are similar (though their slight differences as a literary technique draw us to pay more attention to them). Their repetitiveness underscores the importance of this point: human beings respond with blasphemy to God's efforts to draw them to repentance. They resented the fact that God had the power over these plagues, but, instead of letting his power draw them to his love, they did not repent and give him the glory.

These responses call each one of us to repentance. How easily we resent God's power, instead of seeing that it is always used for the purposes of his love! Sometimes we feel backed into a corner, with no way out except God's way—and we rebel because we don't have more choices. To write this makes me feel ashamed of my stubbornness. How long I have fought some of God's purposes in my life because I keep wanting to do things my way. Even as my husband waited through six years of friendship for me to recognize and accept his devotion and commitment, so God waits infinitely long for the people of the earth to repent and be drawn to his forgiveness and salvation.

The sixth plague, however, makes us realize that God won't wait forever. Finally his judgment must come.

The beginning (16:12) of the description of that plague, however, contains a mysterious little section (as so many in The Revelation) that stirs up our curiosity and invites us to deeper reflection. When the angel pours the bowl, the waters of the great river Euphrates are dried up in order to prepare the way for the kings of the east. The only other use of this phrase "of the east" in The Revelation occurs in chapter 7, just before the sealing of the elect of God. Besides this reminder of God's care, the picture of the Euphrates drying up would remind the original readers of The Revelation of God's promise in Isaiah 11:15–16 and 44:27–28, that the river would be dried up and a way made for his people to return from the Babylonian captivity. Cyrus himself (a king of the east) would be a shepherd to fulfill God's purposes of restoration. Thus, in the midst of these descriptions of the plagues shines another promise that God would gather in his people and care for them.

The plague itself, this sixth and final one, is actually initiated by the powers of evil, for out of the mouths of the dragon, the beast, and the false prophet flow three unclean spirits like frogs, which give us a vivid image of their peskiness, their ability to get around everywhere, their pervasiveness. These, we are told, are the spirits of the demons, the ones who perform signs and who gather the kings of all the world for the war with God.

Our concentration is pulled away from their gathering, however, by the reminder that Christ is coming soon (v. 15). We must pay careful attention to this literary emphasis, which underscores my point about the whole book of Revelation. We ought not to hate the book or be afraid of it, for it does not primarily emphasize gruesome wars and horrible creatures. We are not allowed to focus here on the gathering of the kings for war against God, nor on the evil spirits who call them. Rather, they are gathering for the war "of the great day of God, the Almighty" (v. 14). That phrase resets our bearings, as does verse 15, which reminds us that those who are waiting for the coming of Christ are blessed. They are not naked and ashamed if they are awake and watching. Rather, they will thus have kept their garments to be ready for his coming.

Verse 16 refocuses on the war, and certainly we have all heard various theories about this great battle of Armageddon. During the most critical years of the cold war (before Mikhail Gorbachev's efforts to de-escalate the arms race), some people thought that Armageddon would take place in a nuclear war. Such theories totally miss the point of the name.

The name literally is *Har-mageddon*. The word is an oxymoron, a figure of speech in which contradictory terms are combined. The plain of Megiddo was a famous site for several important battles in Jewish history, so it might have been immediately recognized as a place of conflict by those who first read The Revelation. However, they might also have been taken aback by the prefix *Har*, for that Hebrew word signifies a mountain, whereas the plain of Megiddo is the flattest land in Israel. What could this mean, the Mountain of the Battle Plain?

As with all the imagery of The Revelation, this oxymoron (which might not have even been recognized as such by the original readers) reminds us not to put these illustrations of the conflict of good and evil into literalistic, physical human terms. The book of Revelation is not trying to teach us how the world will end. Rather, it seeks to comfort us in our struggles with the hope that, in the end, evil will ultimately be vanquished forever.

This emphasis is reinforced by the seventh plague, which is depicted with all the elements from the First Testament for a theophany, an appearance of God. Flashes of lightning, peals of thunder, and severe earthquakes all remind us of God's descent to Mount Sinai (which we then connect with the Mount of Megiddo). These images reinforce that the end of the world is not going to be brought about by any warring between the kings of the earth, but by the mighty coming of God. Furthermore, the warring of the kings is not the cause of anything that happens, for the loud voice from the temple has already said that "it has come to pass" (16:17), and the Greek verb tense emphasizes that what has already come to pass remains. God's justice and righteousness have already had their way. Evil was destroyed at the cross, and now we will see effected what Christ already accomplished there.

The images of the next few verses reinforce this point. The cities of the nations fall; God's cup of wrath is poured out on Babylon, which is split in three (v. 19); the islands and mountains flee (v. 20); and huge hailstones fall (v. 21). However, the scene ends (v. 21) with this tragic declaration that the whole picture was meant to make more poignant to us: even though all these events happen to warn human beings and to call them to repentance, still they respond only with more blasphemy. This time the verse does not even contain the comment that they refused to repent. It did not even enter their minds that this was the reason for all their agony.

How terribly disturbing it is if Christians rejoice over a coming Armageddon, almost giddy because God will punish all the evil people in the world. No, instead we must leave this chapter with subdued hearts. How easily we, too, blaspheme God and do not repent. How have I failed to heed his warnings? What call is he giving me now to which I'm not paying heed? In what areas of my life am I being rebellious? Why do I deserve his wrath—and yet know that his grace enfolds me? How can this be, that in my failures and weaknesses and doubts and sinfulness his grace still enfolds me? How can I spread the message of that grace more effectively? How can I urge my neighbors to repent and learn God's love?

It drives me to my knees in gratitude—this overwhelming grace of God!

26

Fallen! Fallen Is Babylon the Great!

Please refer often to Revelation 17–18 as you study this chapter.

One of the most painful narratives in the gospels is the account of the rich man who asked Jesus what he must do to inherit eternal life. In the ensuing discussion Jesus tells him to sell all that he has, to give it to the poor, and to follow him. The rich man walks away, sad and possessed by his possessions. Poignantly, Mark's account includes the important statement, "Jesus looked at him and loved him" (Mark 10:21). How Jesus longed to deliver that rich man from the snare of Mammon! He yearned for him to turn back in repentance and contrition. God delights when his grace leads us to recognize our sin and turn to him in sorrow.

As the Hebrew prophets repeatedly show and as Revelation 17–18 makes clear, the power of Mammon is extremely tenacious. God calls us repeatedly through his Word and his messengers to repent, but eventually he must judge those who reject his grace and continue in their idolatries.

In 1988 sexual scandals surfaced in connection with televangelists Jim Bakker and Jimmy Swaggart. As we Christians face the cynicism of a world that already looks askance at our Christian beliefs, we must realize that these men fell morally long before they were caught in explicit sexual immorality. The demonic power of Mammon had ensnared them.

Consider also the dangers to Christians of becoming enculturated both personally and corporately in the world's economic patterns that are contrary to those of the Gospel. For example, Christians must question our culture's ostentatious weddings, which spend enormous amounts of money for glitz that covers up the biblical focus of marriage. Throughout history various Christian

182

denominations have been characterized by a spirit of accumulation rather than generosity, by exploitation of the Two-Thirds World rather than economic support, by seeking after economic power rather than siding with the poor and the oppressed. Some church bodies recently have reassessed their character, but individuals and movements have questioned Christian economic policies ever since Constantine first joined the church with the Roman empire.

The Hebrew prophets fervently warned Israel of the idolatry of wealth. Jesus warned us, too. About one-sixth of his sayings in the synoptic gospels relate to the problem of the god Mammon. Here The Revelation culminates the warning that economic temptation is the undoing of the world, that the principality we have most to fear is that of Mammon.

Out of all the judgments depicted by the bowls of wrath, chapters 17 and 18 focus on the particular judgment of the city Babylon. Of course, this name does not refer only to that specific city, for it has stood throughout the Scriptures as the name for those who oppress God's people. To the original readers of The Revelation, it stood for Rome, but Jacques Ellul makes an effective argument for understanding Babylon as the archetypal city, the focus of sin, one of the powers that exerts its influence on the present world.[1]

At first we might think that the city's greatest problem is its sexual immorality, because the angel summoned the seer to show him the great harlot, "with whom the kings of the earth committed sexual immorality." However, the First Testament set the biblical precedent for using the title "harlot" to denote more than sexual immorality; especially Hosea in his life and words repeatedly warned Israel against going "awhoring after other gods." Now the entire description of Revelation 17 and 18 exposes the treacherous lure of Mammon's luxury and economic injustice.

The beast on which the harlot sits is full of blasphemous names and has symbols of authority and power in the perfect and complete numbers (7 heads and 10 horns). This reminder of the first beast (from Rev. 14) points to the demonic power that produces its influence on the world through her.

The beginning description of the harlot herself unveils her excessive luxury. She is clothed in purple and scarlet and adorned with gold, precious stones, and pearls—all symbols in the ancient world of wealth. Her cup is gold, and it is full of her abominations, her uncleanness and immorality.

Two other things we must notice about her at this point. First, her name is very complete and seemingly self-explanatory—"Babylon the Great, the Mother of Harlots and of the Abominations of the Earth" (17:5 NASB)—and yet it is specifically called a mystery. That word warns us not to think that we can pin her title down, that we can reduce it to some simplistic understanding. She does not merely stand for Rome (in the time of The Revelation) or some decadent city in our present age. Evil pervades everything. We dare not think it is only focalized in a particular city, race of people, or type of sin.

Second, she was drunk with the blood of the saints and the witnesses of Jesus. Many Christians throughout history have lost their lives in battle against the power of Mammon. Consider, for example, the many martyrs in Central and South American countries whose Christian faith directed their work among the poor and powerless and led to their arrest and torture or assassination. Moreover, there is no point to giving in even slightly to this world's powers in the hopes that we can preserve our own life. As believers in eastern Europe and the former Soviet Union found out, raw Mammon kills Christians, including those who try to accommodate. It even happens here in the United States to employees of integrity who refuse to obey criminal business practices, although the "killing" usually takes a less obvious form. (We are also warned by these chapters to be vigilant against, and to continue to resist, extreme luxury, which leads to economic injustice that actually kills.)

At the seer's wondering (17:6), the angel proceeds to tell him all about the mysteries of the woman and the beast (vv. 7–18). Various interpretations of this story have falsely pinned down its details, greatly to the destruction of its point.

It is true that, for the first people who read this book, the description in the text most likely raised up various associations with the city of Rome, and we do well to locate its initial meaning there. However, the danger is to take that kind of specific identification into the future and declare that we can associate these descriptions with particular people and places in the 20th century (identifying, for example, the 10 kings with the European Common Market). In doing so, we violate major rules for reading the Bible.

Our procedure throughout this book has been to locate the meaning of a text in its history at the time of writing, when the Christians were being persecuted by Imperial Rome and needed hope and comfort. For today, however, that kind of geographical locating is not possible, for there are Christians everywhere being persecuted by all kinds of governments. We have become a global community, and our persecutors sometimes are people who claim the heritage of a "Christian nation." We need, therefore, to note the sins of which the harlot is guilty, to see how those sins have pervaded our lives, and to be called to repentance and new strength to stand against the powers that draw us to false values and actions.

The very language of 17:8–18 makes us realize that we run into trouble if we reduce the image to only one specific figure. The beast is drawn as the "one who was and is not, and is about to come" These phrases remind us of the parody in chapters 13 and 14, in which the powers of evil imitate the God "who is, who was, and who is to come," a description by which he is named throughout The Revelation. This particular scarlet beast, whose heads are various kings, might represent any demonic line of government or dynasty of emperors.

The seven kings, of which five have fallen, probably referred originally to specific Roman emperors (since Rome sat on seven hills), but that very identification warns us against trying to match them up with specific people now in order to calendarize the end of the world. Instead, the situation in first-century Rome shows us this tendency: the principalities and powers of the earth rise and fall.

The language of 17:10–11 is quite mysterious, though it probably had specific connotations for the original readers of The Revelation. Consider "the beast which was and is not, is himself also an eighth, and is one of the seven" (v. 11 NASB). This power of evil manifests itself in particular forms in our world, yet it is a principality outside of human influences. Though we do not know the particular identifications, we can certainly know that the beast is headed for destruction. We saw in chapter 14 that the beast is an imitation of God, that the demonic principalities usurp a power that is not theirs. We must be wary of all the forms that these principalities take in our modern world.[2]

Five essential items of the description that closes Revelation 17 must be noted. First of all, these kings and powers all receive their authority from someone else (v. 12). They serve one purpose, and that is to give power to the beast. All the evil influences in our world serve one end—to contradict and destroy the work of God and to draw humankind away from God. Ultimately, as The Revelation repeatedly shows us, there is but this one conflict in the cosmos: between the purposes of God and the purposes of Satan.

Second, none of these kings, beasts, horns, and whatever are going to be able to accomplish anything in the end (v. 14). They might seem to cause a lot of trouble now, to get all sorts of people to live under their sway and to act on their power. In the final war against the Lamb, however, he will overcome them all because, let us never forget, he is Lord over every lord and King of all kings and everything else.

Third, wonder of wonders! We are named right there with him. The ones with the Lamb are the "called and chosen and faithful." These names appear repeatedly in The Revelation and throughout the entire New Testament. They give us enormous hope for the future. The Lamb who will ultimately triumph keeps us securely right by his side. We are not going to be left behind. He has called us; he has chosen us; and by the power of His Spirit, we are faithful in response to his grace.

Fourth, an awful lot of people get sucked up into the deceptions of the powers (v. 15). Again, a fourplex (peoples, multitudes, nations, and tongues) summarizes the universality of their influence. The four corners of the earth and everything else in between are harassed by the workings of the powers. No place on earth escapes the demonic working of the forces of evil.

However, none of this is out of God's control. Verse 16 reminds us of this final point: the powers of evil betray and destroy themselves. The 10 horns and the beast turn on the harlot, just as those lusting for power in our world make use of people only until they are no longer needed and then turn their machinations against them. The manipulation and exploitation of one another always characterizes the demonic powers and their cohorts. Ultimately, however, even these demonic turnings accomplish the purposes of God. Evil wreaks its own havoc; God's righteous wrath and punishment allow evil eventually to annihilate itself.

From the perspective of Christ's victory, evil is indeed already destroyed; but, until his victory is thoroughly manifested at the end of the world, evil continues to carry within itself the seeds of its own abolition. God's purposes of good cannot be thwarted—the last enemies were exposed and defeated in the cross and resurrection of Jesus. That is why chapter 18 begins with the declaration that Babylon *has* fallen. The angel announces God's judgment that Babylon has doomed herself because many participate in her sins (specifically the acts of sexual immorality and the excessive luxury of her sensuality) and because she is a dwelling place for evil powers. The angel who bears this message is described in a way that underscores his authority, namely, even the earth is illumined with the glory of that authority.

Chapter 18 is self-explanatory. After the declaration of the reasons for the harlot's fall (vv. 1–3), there is another call to repentance (v. 4). People are urged to come away from the sins with which she is imbued. They are warned not to participate in her iniquities and sensuality, for she will surely be tormented to the degree that she has glorified herself and lived without concern for others (vv. 6–7).

Note again the point made earlier, that her major sin is not so much sexual immorality as the sensuality of wealth. Notice the long lists of kinds of luxury related to the city. All the rest of chapter 18 is composed of various elements that make up the god of Mammon: luxury goods, exploitation of other human beings, sensual pleasures, empty hilarity, self-absorption in music and crafts and festivals—all without any concern for the call of God.

The text, of course, is not criticizing music or crafts, cinnamon or ivory, money or parties *per se*. What are denounced are the deception, the greedy amassing of material possessions, hilarity without meaning, self-aggrandizement without care for the rest of the world, the killing of the saints, and the idolatries.

Perhaps our age has made up so many interpretations of The Revelation because we have not wanted to face how much this 18th chapter condemns us. In a world of gross inequities, *we* are reproached for our accumulation of silver and silks and spices. *We* are rebuked for our enculturation into a society that has fallen to the power of Mammon. We dare not read The Revelation to find out whom to blame as having 10 heads. We can only read it to know our own sin and to repent for it with humility and grief.

The Revelation is not a book for the mighty—who think they are better than others because they have not fallen to the sin of sexual immorality, like those prominent Christians caught in scandals. It is a book for the weak, for those who know they have fallen and need redemption and grace.

Notes

1. See Jacques Ellul's *The Meaning of the City*, trans. Dennis Pardee (Grand Rapids, MI: Wm. B. Eerdmans Publishing Co., 1970), for his very powerful argument and warning.
2. Many of Jacques Ellul's works discuss the biblical concept of the principalities and powers and their contemporary manifestations and influences. See especially *The Humiliation of the Word*, trans. Joyce Main Hanks (Grand Rapids: Wm. B. Eerdmans Publishing Co., 1985); and *Money and Power*, trans. LaVonne Neff (Downers Grove, IL: InterVarsity Press, 1984).

27

Preludes and Wedding Songs

Please refer often to Revelation 19:1–10 as you study this chapter.

After the wild frenzy and deathly darkness of the storm, the brilliantly hued double rainbow was all the more beautiful. In contrast to the wracking pain of the day before, the genuine calmness in my body was most refreshing. After the frantic pace of the previous day's activities, the leisure and pleasant visiting of my Sabbath Day was a welcomed relief. Many of the positive experiences of our lives are made all the more delectable by the dichotomous contrast between them and what proceeded them.

In Revelation 19, the virtues of the bride, viewed from a heavenly perspective, are made all the more magnificent by the extreme contrast to the harlot of the previous chapters, who was viewed from the perspectives of earth. Whereas the harlot was characterized by sin, corruption, mourning, doom, death, and sorrow, the bride is portrayed as righteousness, purity, singing, victory, life, and Joy. Also, the series of three laments about the doom of the city Babylon (chapter 18) is contrasted now with the three songs of praise and victory at the beginning of chapter 19 (vv. 1–3, 4, and 5).

As another contrast, the elders and the living creatures, who again appear in 19:4, vanish after this incident. All along they have served to point to the Lamb, and in the process we grow rather fond of those characters in the drama. However, their disappearance from the scene is necessary at this point so that full attention can be given for the rest of the book to the final victory of the Lamb and his marriage with the bride. In order for us to appreciate the immensity of the victory, all elements of the story now point to it rather than to other characters who have participated in the drama thus far.

There is also great dramatic splendor in the announcing of the marriage feast. The addition of such elements as the voice of the great crowd, like the sound of many waters (images from Ezek. 1:24 and 43:2) or the loud peals of thunder (Dan. 10:6), heighten our anticipation for the announcement that will proclaim the Lamb's feast.

As another example of God's delightful timing, while first writing this chapter on the thundering voices, I was enjoying the sounds of a good old Midwestern thunderstorm. I grew up liking them, probably because my mother had first calmed me with the assurance that the thunder was the voice of God. (On days when I'd been really naughty that was a rather terrifying thought, but on most days of my childhood the idea of God's loving voice was comforting.) Now living on the West Coast, I have sorely missed the strong thunderstorms, so I thoroughly enjoyed the crashes and drummings of the storm while working on this chapter. This experience served, as does Revelation 19:6, to heighten my anticipation as we prepare for the grand finale of the book of Revelation.

All of this noise in chapter 19 proclaims a momentous change of perspective. For several chapters The Revelation has focused on the corruption of Babylon and the way she has corrupted the earth. Anyone not in touch with the reality of sin will grasp it easily if he or she pays attention to the evil described in these chapters. Now in 19:2–4 the fall of Babylon is announced and praised.

We must be careful, however, to note in the praise of verse 2 a critical distinction between our humanly marred revenge and God's righteous condemnation. The great harlot is not destroyed "to get even." Rather, God's vengeance on the city comes from his "true and just" judgments. With total holiness and truth God condemns the great prostitute and vindicates his people by avenging their death.

We must be very fearful of liberation (or any other) theologies that resort to violence and power. When they do so, the motive for victory seems to become revenge rather than restoration of God's true justice. We cannot justify violence as a means to an end, for the character of the end must also determine the means. We won't restore truth if we use false means to attain it; if our goals are peace and justice in the world, we will not bring them about by methods that are unjust or inflict pain on others.

My friend Linden provides a good model of this correlation of means and ends for asserting truth. I have never seen in him any violence against others; he is not capable of it. Rather, he accomplishes his purposes by gentle forbearance and careful suffering. I call it "careful" because it is not masochistic. We do not choose to suffer, just for suffering's sake, if it is not necessary. However, if our faithfulness to the plan of God involves suffering, then we willingly bear that cross of suffering for the purposes of the kingdom.

The many references in The Revelation to Babylon's corrupting influence on the kings of the earth (see 14:8; 17:2; and 18:3) show the great extent to which her evil has been perpetrated and why the salvation the triumphant believers experience is such a great source of Joy. The final "Amen, Hallelujah" of the elders and beasts (19:4) reinforces this image, especially because the phrase echoes Psalm 106:48, which marks the end of the fourth book of the Psalter and serves as the climax of a tremendous poem proclaiming the ways in which the LORD has taken note of the distresses of his people and restored them in remembrance of his covenant with them.

Revelation 19:5–10 ties together several main points of the New Testament. The passage talks about praise, celebration, equality, blessedness, rejoicing, the righteous deeds of the saints, and the purity of the bride.

One aspect of this chapter of The Revelation that is especially important in light of the purposes of this book is the equality mentioned at several points. In verse 5, the great voice declares that all bondservants of God are to praise him, both the great and the small. Later, when the seer John falls at the feet of the angel to worship, the latter reprimands him with these words: "Do not do that; I am a fellow-servant of yours" and of the brothers and sisters (19:10 NASB). All of us together are servants (literally in the Greek, "slaves") out of love for the Lord; all of us equally need to praise him; no one among us deserves honor, for all the glory belongs to God and to him alone. Everything else is reduced to equality— even angels and humankind—because of the surpassing magnificence of the Lord's greatness.

All the servants of God are invited to participate in the celebration and the praising, for, as was announced in 19:6, the Lord our God has indeed reigned. Though most English translations render this verb in the present tense ("reigns"), the original Greek verb is in the past tense. The difference is important, for the past tense proclaims that the Christ has been Lord even when that was not apparent. His was the triumph even before we saw the destruction of Babylon. Therefore, we can rejoice and be glad and give him the glory because the wedding feast of the Lamb has come and his bride has prepared herself.

The expression "rejoice and be glad" (v. 7) occurs in only one other place in the New Testament—in Matthew 5:12, where the cause for such rejoicing is the greatness of the heavenly reward awaiting those who have been reviled and persecuted for the cause of Christ. That passage in Matthew occurs at the end of the Beatitudes. Here in The Revelation the expression is followed by the fourth of the seven beatitudes in this book (1:3; 14:13; 16:15; 19:9; 20:6; and 22:7, 14).

We must also notice that Revelation 19 stresses the purity of the Lamb's bride, since the Scriptures elsewhere focus more on the bride's failure (especially in the book of the prophet Hosea, where the bride Israel is represented by his prostituting wife, Gomer). Nevertheless, as Hosea 3:1 shows, the Lord promises a husband's protection and care to his recalcitrant bride, the people of Israel (cf. also Is. 54:5–7). Of course, the well-known portrait of Ephesians 5:22–33 gives the most positive image of the bride of Christ.

The bride in Revelation 19, however, is dressed in white linens (v. 8), which are defined as the righteous deeds of the saints. We must read that description in the light of the whole chapter, lest we think that those righteous deeds earn her salvation. All the other images of the context—the victory of God over the corruption of the harlot, the rejoicing and blessedness given to the saints in this celebration—are very important, for they prevent us from creating a false conflict in this passage between faith and obedience. Rather, the true church is obedient in her faith, and a submissive church is faithful in that obedience. Verse 8 does not deny justification by grace, but it stresses instead that a transformed life is the proper response to the call of the bridegroom.

A similar combination of the truths of justification and sanctification is found in Ephesians 2:8–10, where the great hymn about faith being a gift (and definitely not of works lest anyone might boast) is followed by the assertion that we are God's workmanship, created to do the good works he has designed beforehand in order that we might walk in them. Here the picture is the same: the linen garments have been prepared for the bride. She definitely puts them on and is involved in the righteous deeds that God has planned, but they are not the works of her own creation.

How blessed to participate, then, in the marriage feast. We are reminded of the great parable of Jesus (Matt. 22:2–14) in which he declares that, when those who have been invited refuse to come, the Lord of the supper invites all the lame and blind and helpless from the roadsides to come to the feast. All are made welcome, except the one who has refused to accept the wedding garment that would have been provided for him if he had not rejected it.

Once again the importance of our own weakness is emphasized. God doesn't invite us to the feast because we are worthy; we cannot come out of our own capabilities. Rather, we truly come to the wedding supper when, out of our helplessness, we joyfully receive the gifts of God's gracious banquet.

As we, along with the seer John, recognize our humble station, we too would fall to worship the angel who has brought the good news of the supper, but the angel continues to remind us that we are all equally servants who need to direct all our worship to God and not to each other. It is the testimony of Jesus that must always draw forth our response of praise.

Often the main emphasis of self-proclaimed "miracle workers" is on what they have done. They dress with finery and live in luxury and proclaim the wonders of God working through *them*. On the other hand, those who faithfully follow Jesus in the sufferings of illness offer a significant contrast to these faith healers who try to "fix" them. The former give better testimony to Jesus in their humble submission to God's best purposes, even including suffering.

Notice again the theocentrism of it all. We can truly know our place only when we are focused on the Lord's glory and recognize his preeminence.

That is illustrated graphically in 19:11–16, the picture of the warrior going forth to the final battle (which we have already considered in chapter 17). He is described in terms of majesty and carries the title of the faithful and the true. Notice the emphasis on his justice with which he both judges and fights. All that he does is eminently right.

Again, as in chapter 1, his eyes are described as flames of fire, and he is crowned with many crowns and an unknowable name. He is also called the Word, and he leads the armies of the hosts of heaven to engage in the last battle against the evil opposition that has controlled the world till the end. And now the great and final destruction of the enemies of God will begin.

The overall literary construction of this segment is dramatic. The great destruction of the harlot Babylon is proclaimed, the bride of the Lamb is introduced, and the wedding supper is announced before the final scene of battle in order that we might anticipate the victory as well as participate in it.

Such an expectation has dominated the whole book of Revelation. All along we have known that God would be the triumphant Lord. Though we have agonized over the persecution of the saints and the opposition of all the satanic forces, yet all along we have known the assurance of the victory. The bride has been getting ready. In the hymns of praise throughout the book, we have acknowledged the reign of God and looked forward to its consummation.

This is the attitude that prevails in a theology of weakness. In spite of the sufferings of the present moment, in which all of us are reduced to equality before the Lord whom we worship together, we have tasted of the final victory. And that gives us courage to put up with the pain of the meanwhile.

28

The Ultimate Defeat of the Powers of Evil and the Present Reign of Christ

Please refer often to Revelation 20:1–21:8 as you study this chapter.

There are a lot of things that I (stupidly) worry about, but what I should do when having an insulin reaction is not one of them. The first time I ever had one I was terrified, not understanding why my body was suddenly becoming so uncoordinated and clammy. I was a teenager, formerly very athletic and active, but suddenly I became a diabetic because of the destructive effects of a measles virus. I rang for the nurse and anxiously explained to her my symptoms. She calmly introduced me to the reasons for, and treatment of, insulin reactions. My fear of them was pretty well killed that day.

I hate them. I want like crazy to avoid them. However, I don't have to fear them as I did that first day because I know that what I need is a good dose of sugar—and fast!

That illustration is, of course, totally inadequate to describe the meaning of the first and second death, but it is a simple case in which, having conquered the fear when a reaction occurs, I no longer have to be alarmed. The nurse's patient instruction freed me to go into my future with insulin without terror about what to do when my dosage isn't right.

Any illustration would be inadequate. Incredibly more powerful is the freedom of those who have a part in the first resurrection and, therefore, will not have to fear the second death, for it can have no power over them (Rev. 20:6). This verse is the key for our understanding the difficult problem of the 1,000-year reign of Christ in the book of Revelation, and it will help us better to understand the ultimate defeat of Satan.

The 20th chapter of The Revelation causes much trouble because too often the number 1,000 is understood in a literalistic sense. All the other numbers in the book are symbolic numbers, and surely this one is, too. Ten (the complete number) multiplied by itself three times (the divine number) certainly emphasizes that this 1,000-year reign is divinely complete. However, what does it mean that Christ will reign for 1,000 years? We simply must understand the phrase properly because otherwise we forfeit the Joy that can be ours in experiencing in the present his sovereign reign already begun. We can delight in it now already, even though there is still pain and suffering in the world.

Often our struggles with limitations help us to understand the presence of his reign more thoroughly than when everything seems to go well for us. When we suffer horrible afflictions, we might believe at first that evil will overcome us. Then in the midst of affliction we discover, by God's gracious provision, that Christ rules and that the evil, though terrifyingly imminent, cannot overcome us.

Now in the final revisions of this book, I am presently going through such a learning time. After almost 30 health complications in the past dozen years (including a bowel resectioning and a foot reconstruction, frequent unhealable wounds inside my leg brace and bouts with intestinal disorders, a hysterectomy, and several surgeries on my hands and eyes), I was finally able to walk and see again—only to discover lumps that were cancerous. My first reaction was to scream, "God, it isn't fair! I've had more than my share of physical suffering!" At that moment, I needed God's reminders that evil cannot overcome us. And those reminders came—in the truths of The Revelation as I worked on this book; in other Scripture readings, hymns, and sermons; in the care and cards of friends; in the flowers in the yard and the beauty of creation; and mostly in the Lenten worship services that reveal God's love on the cross to triumph over all the powers of evil, the enemies of suffering and death.

The apostle Paul knew profound suffering, too, and asked God to deliver him, but, after receiving the assurance from God that grace would always be sufficient, he learned that evil cannot ulti- mately overcome us. He declares this triumphantly in one of my favorite parts of his second letter to the Corinthians. After noting that we hold a treasure in old clay pots to show that the transcendent power belongs to God and not to us, he describes the near miss of Satan's wiles against us in these terms:

> We are afflicted in every way, but not crushed; perplexed, but not despairing; persecuted, but not forsaken; struck down, but not destroyed. 2 Cor. 4:8–9 NASB

J. B. Phillips paraphrases these verses in this way:

> We are handicapped on all sides, but we are never frustrated; we are puzzled, but never in despair. We are persecuted, but we never have to stand it alone; we may be knocked down, but we are never knocked out!

Sometimes the more tightly we get hemmed in, the more we learn of God's lordship over it all. During a horrible period several years ago when I was allergic to insulin and woke up in the middle of night after night with severe insulin reactions, I had a deep sense of God's protection and care. What if I hadn't awakened and my blood sugar had continued to plummet so far below the line that I couldn't have ever awakened? Who would have found me? Such questions crossed my mind—and yet each time the Lord woke me up. In the affliction I rejoiced that I was never physically or emotionally crushed.

Similarly, one of the most joyful times of my life occurred during a period of being teased and persecuted for my Christian beliefs. My faith was strengthened more at that time than ever before, and I delighted to see God at work in the situation that developed. Those who harassed me most became more open to the good news of the Gospel. Meanwhile, members of a Bible study group I was leading gave me strong support, and the experience of such Christian community showed me that, though persecuted, I was never spiritually abandoned.

It is this sense of God's sovereignty—in spite of evidence to the contrary—that is underscored by the message of The Revelation concerning the reign of Christ and the ultimate defeat of the evil powers. At the end of the 19th chapter, the false prophet and the beast are thrown into the lake of fire, and the armies of heaven wage war against all the kings of the earth and their forces of evil. They are victorious by means of the sword of the Word.

In spite of such certainty, the binding of Satan for 1,000 years (Rev. 20:2) leads people to question whether this occurs before or after the tribulation, before or after the Second Coming of Christ, and so forth. However, the symbolism and mystery of The Revelation cannot be pinned down chronologically and literalistically. When we read Revelation 20 very carefully, we learn all that can be known about the eventual triumph of God's reign. The most important aspect is when that ultimate victory begins.

The chronological key lies in the combination of two verses that bracket and structure the text literarily and theologically:

> Blessed and holy is the one who has a part in the first resurrection; over these the second death has no power, but they will be priests of God and of Christ and will reign with Him for a thousand years (20:6 NASB).

> But for the cowardly and unbelieving and abominable and murderers and immoral persons and sorcerers and idolaters and all liars, their part will be in the lake that burns with fire and brimstone, which is the second death (21:8 NASB).

These two statements structure very clearly a theology that recognizes the reign of Christ beginning at his (the first) resurrection and continuing until the end of time when the second death finally separates his own from those who have rejected him. That sequence is developed in Revelation 20 and 21.

The first essential point in this theology is that God's reign was instituted in the cross and resurrection of Christ. The New Testament frequently proclaims Christ's triumph in his crucifixion over the powers of separation, death, and Satan. (See Eph. 2:13–16 and Col. 2:13–15.) Furthermore, the reign of the saints is declared in 1 Peter 2:5 and 9, as well as earlier in Revelation 1:6 and 5:10. Moreover, the apostle Paul constantly stresses that believers participate in Christ's death and resurrection and thereby reign with him. (See Gal. 2:20 and Rom. 8:9–11, as well as Eph. 2:4–6.)

Of course, Christ does not yet show his reign over everything and everyone. However, it began when, on the cross, he defeated the political, economic, and even religious principalities and powers and when he burst from the tomb triumphant over the last enemy, death. His present rule is evident in the fact that since his resurrection the Gospel has continued to draw people to Christ and to spread hope and faith throughout the world. Indeed, he is already making his people into participants in his reign. Those who have been martyred for the gospel, for example, are assured that their sacrifice was not in vain, but that they actually share in Christ's reign during this time. Those who are not God's people do not partake in Christ's resurrection. Meanwhile, one of the marks of the times is that Satan does not have ultimate power to deceive the nations. He was bound by Christ on the cross and will try, at the end of time, to gather the world for war against God, but he will immediately be defeated and cast into the lake of fire (20:3–10).

These verses in Revelation 20 circle around the basic fact that God's people are secure in his sovereignty even though Satan will do his utmost to wage war against God. Those who participate with Christ in the first resurrection do not have to fear the second death at the end of time when all the powers of evil are destroyed. We know that there will ultimately be a final showdown at the end of the world in which the forces of Satan will be totally devoured and the devil himself perpetually tormented. What we do not know is the timing of that final defeat.

It will indeed be ultimate. Furthermore, the defeat will be accomplished entirely by God's hand. Notice that the text says the enemy will surround God's people, but the former will be annihilated by fire that will come down from heaven (20:9).

Too many branches of Christianity try to prepare for the last battle as if there were anything we mere humans could do about it. At the height of the cold war, some wanted to stockpile nuclear arms to prepare for the Armageddon of a third world war. This theology was usually coupled with the notion that we must possess the power to demolish the enemies of God—namely, the U.S.S.R. Such an attitude has no basis in the biblical account (and did not take into consideration the millions of God's people living in "enemy" lands). *God's* fire (20:9), not ours, will destroy the enemy. True, his people are surrounded, but in their weakness they will experience the ultimate triumph.

Verse 11 introduces the scene of judgment. Because of this sequence, it makes more sense to understand the reign of Christ as happening now. Satan has been bound so that he is not in complete control, but his cohorts are still at work causing trouble in the world. Then, when Satan is released for his final fling (which is cut short by the fire of God to destroy his forces), all that has taken place in this meanwhile time will be judged. Those who have rejected God and lived according to evils of the 666 will be brought up from death and hell and Hades and finally be thrown into the lake of fire. At that point—the time of the judgment, the second death—all evil will be totally obliterated from the presence of those whose names are written in the book of life.

Next, chapter 21 promises the new heaven and the new earth— a heaven and earth unmarred by the presence of any of the powers of evil, for they have all been thrown into the lake of fire. This is especially emphasized in the text by the assertion that there is no longer any sea, for earlier in The Revelation (13:1) the sea was associated with the dragon and his beasts. Already in the First Testament the sea had symbolized the powers of evil. Since there were no natural harbors along the Israelite coastline, the Jews had never become much of a seafaring people. No wonder that to them the sea represented terror and death.

Now we see the heavenly Jerusalem, prepared as a bride beautifully adorned for her husband (21:2). Throughout our study of the seer's vision, we must remember that he is not describing the new Jerusalem as a *place*, but as a metaphor for the people of God, in whose midst God will someday dwell. Previously the old city of Zion metaphorically stood for the whole people of Israel, who longed for the coming of the Messiah, while the temple represented and demonstrated the presence of God. Now the new Jerusalem encompasses all the believers, and, most wonderful of all, the tabernacling of God with his people is announced as an actual reality (21:3). (Remember that in Rev. 7:15 it was still seen as a future hope. Refer to our discussion in chapter 18.)

In God's eternal presence everything is new, and all that is associated with evil is done away with forever. Tears and suffering and pain will not have a place when God is with his people, for the old order, these first things, will have passed away (21:4–5).

Because the old order had not been demolished during the 1,000-year reign, we can't postulate a millennium only at the end of time when the reign of Christ is complete. It is an already-but-not-yet reign, taking place now, during which the old order still continues to exist, though it cannot have ultimate authority because Satan himself has been bound. However, he has not yet been totally defeated—that remains for the end of time—so he and his under-demons are still continuing to wreak their havoc in the world.

Eagerly we look forward to the time when God says, "It is done." He is the beginning and the end, and someday he will ful-fill his promise of drink to all who are thirsty (notice again these images from Isaiah). Furthermore, God promises all these gifts as an inheritance to those who overcome (a phrase reminding us of all the promises given in the seven letters in Rev. 2–3). The overcom-ers will be God's sons (with all the rights and privileges that sonship signified in the first century), for indeed God will be their God.

When the old order passes away, however, all that is of the old order will no longer have any place. Those who have backed down from the faith (the cowardly), those who have rejected the faith (the unbelieving), and those who have not accepted the wholeness of salvation in its power to transform our lifestyle (the abominable, the murderers, the immoral persons, the magicians, the idolaters, and the liars) will not have a place in the new order. They will be destroyed by the second death (21:8).

On the other hand, those who have participated in the resur-rection—to use Paul's terms, those who have died with Christ and, thereby, have died to sin and risen to new life in him—will not be harmed by this second death. This death does away instead with all that is related to sin.

The list of those persons who will be harmed by the second death not only speaks of the time of judgment and ultimate defeat of evil, but also gives us an urgent warning. To participate in the kingdom of God is to resist the temptation to engage in such atti-tudes and activities. Modern Christians must pay more careful heed to all the aspects of this warning.

We can see by the combination of sins on the list that no dimen-sion of our ethics is trivial. We would probably all readily agree that those who are idolaters should be cast out of the kingdom and into the lake of fire, but we might wonder if lying is so terribly wrong. This text indicates that it is. So is sexual immorality—and murdering of all kinds, including the many times that we murder each other with snide words and rude glances and violent attitudes and hostile actions.

If we meditate on this text with utmost seriousness, we will each find aspects of our present behavior opposed to the kingdom's principles. Sins of distorting the truth, for example, are just as destructive of God's purposes as other idolatries, such as greed or the sin of killing someone.

I have been especially troubled the last 20 years by the terrible increase of sexual immorality in our culture and the related symptoms of broken marriages, abortions, children growing up without nurture, fractured homes, and juvenile delinquents. So many of these problems feed into each other and multiply the effects of each other. Moreover, many of the problems stem from this same root: a blatant rejection of the authority of God over our bodily life. Those who think they can do what they please with their sexuality are shaking their fist at God's plan in creation and his design for committed relationships. These sins are terribly destructive, yet Christians often do not stand firmly enough against them. The Revelation's warning about the second death and its invitation to participate in the present reign of Christ and the future of his kingdom after the judgment force us to think carefully about our personal and social ethics. The Christian community continually seeks God's guidance for faithfully living out the reign of Christ's kingdom at this time.

His present reign will last for the perfect length of time—completion (10) times itself a divine number (3) of times. It began at the cross and the empty tomb, where Christ defeated the powers, and will continue until the final assault and defeat of Satan. In the meanwhile, however, we manifest Christ's reign to the world by living out the purposes of his kingdom. Because he has made us priests in that kingdom and has enabled us to rule in it, we are invited to be models of that alternative lifestyle right now. Believers in Christ are a people who are marked not with the 666 of idolatrous evil, but with the sign of the Father's name on our foreheads. We must always be asking ourselves if the reign of Christ is evident in all that we are and say and do and choose.

I ponder this question with great sadness. We are all sinners, subject to temptation; we easily let idolatries control our lives. Various immoralities and murders are constant temptations to us. However, we constantly seek to be faithful to God's best purposes because we know that the reign of Christ has begun in our lives and that the Holy Spirit within us empowers us to demonstrate the kingdom's values and purposes in our everyday existence.

I want the reign of Christ to dominate the way I choose, the values I espouse, the behaviors that characterize my lifestyle, the methods that I use to build peace in the world. I want to participate in the 1,000-year, divinely perfect reign as much as possible. Moments when that reign is not evidenced in my life are my fault.

Those Christians who focus on a literal 1,000-year reign of Christ at some time in the future—though all the numbers in The Revelation are symbolic and though Christ tells us we can't know anything about the future calendar—miss the whole message of this section of The Revelation. It clearly calls us to recognize the reign of Christ in this time so that we more deliberately choose to live out the purposes of his kingdom in daily life.

To understand his reign as a present (though not completed) reality makes a huge difference in our perspective on life. We do not have to be defensive about our faith because we will remember that we are already involved in his kingdom and its rule. We will instead seek to live according to the principles of the kingdom in every aspect of our lives and to invite others into the Joy of Christ's present reign.

Such a perspective will influence the way we handle all of our daily affairs—our sexual ethics, our avoidance of magic arts and lies, our desire not to murder anyone with words or actions. Everything that we are and do becomes an important indication of whether or not the lifestyle of the kingdom characterizes our existence and choices.

Most important, Christ's present reign enables us to be overcomers in our times of suffering and trouble. When we feel the force of the assaults of evil—in sickness or doubts or any other sort of spiritual pain—we will cherish the unfailing hope that someday this old order will have passed away. Someday our tears will be gone, so in the meanwhile we can carry on.

29

The Beautiful City:
An Agent of Healing

Please refer often to Revelation 21:9–22:7 as you study this chapter.

One time I received the gift of a plane ticket from Indiana to the state of Washington to spend some restful time with my secretary and her family. As the plane circled around the city of Seattle, my heart soared with the love of that place. How beautiful the city seemed to me, more captivating than ever before! Of course, my ecstasy was deeper because its source was in the unexpected gift of being with people I loved.

Indeed, absence makes the heart grow fonder. Expectant longing deepens our pleasure. For that reason those who struggle with physical limitations or other trials often long more for the beauty of heaven than those who are well and who are so thoroughly involved in the things of this life that they do not want to give up what they are doing now to go to a better life.

Another time, Tim and I were talking about the depth of love in our friendship, and he suddenly said, "I wonder what our friendship will be like in 10 years." I answered that I probably wouldn't live that long, and he responded, "I probably won't either. Just imagine what our friendship will be like in heaven!" What an exciting thought! At last we will have enough time to do all the talking for which we yearn. At last we won't struggle any more with low blood pressures that make us faint and with deficiencies that debilitate our bones and nerves. Most important, at last we will know Jesus face-to-face. How thrilling to look forward to heaven, where all is beautiful to the extreme!

Revelation 21–22 portrays the bride of Christ with such glory that we hardly need to comment on the various dimensions of her beauty. We need no special theological expertise to see in the description a poet gone crazy with delight in all the loveliness of this vision. (I even began to write poetry for the first time in a long while as our plane swooped over Puget Sound and the city of Seattle spread its panorama before my weeping eyes.) However, several characteristics of the city's glorious fulfillment of God's great promises to us are lessons desperately needed in our churches and community relationships.

First of all, we note that the holy city comes down from God and shines with his glory. In other words, the beauty is derived. Nothing inherently worthy in the people of God makes them fit to be the bride of Christ, but we are transformed by his relationship with us and made into the jewel that The Revelation describes.

This emphasis is underscored by the frequent use of the symbolic number 12 in these verses, for it always stands for the people of God. God had made the 12 tribes of Israel his people by his special election and not because they were worthy. They were a weak nation, not very successful, and not large in number, yet God chose them to call them his own (see, for example, Deut. 7:7–8). The derivative nature of our beauty as his people is an important part of our future—and of the present.

The more we recognize the derivative beauty with which God endows us, the more thoroughly we can enjoy it now and appreciate it properly. There is no place for pride in the church, for all that our communities accomplish is by the hand of God among us and through us. When we recognize that his hand is really there, we can find greater worth in all the participants in our community. We can learn more deeply to value the weak and infirm among us, those that the world would call not beautiful, because we can see the beauty in them that God bestows—already, though not yet fully.

Quite mistakenly, some modern biblical translations and paraphrases try to put the measurements of the Holy City into literalistic modern figures. Changing the stadia into miles or kilometers, however, drops the significance of the number 12,000—a number that represents the people of God (12) times completion (10) multiplied by itself a divine number of times (3). Furthermore, the thickness of the wall is 144 cubits or 12 times 12—a doubly reinforced emphasis that this is indeed the city of God's people. Moreover, throughout history walls have been constructed for protection and security. Such a 12 x 12 wall, then, suggests God's great care for his people, his thorough protection and possession. To modernize that figure into 216 feet or 72 yards (as Today's English Version, the New American Standard Version, and the Living Bible do) makes the wall seem ludicrous.

Notice again the use of all kinds of precious stones (some of which can't even be precisely identified anymore) and the predominance of gold and pearl. This piling up of splendid images gives us the opportunity to enter with the seer into his attempt to comprehend a beauty that is not comprehensible. How could we describe that which is beyond description? It's somewhat like when I try to tell people how wonderful my husband is. Words fail me, though, so I always have to end lamely, "You should meet him; then you would understand how gracious he is." Even so, we can hardly begin to imagine the incredible beauty of the presence of God until we get to the place he has prepared for us.

Through all of this someone might object, "But this is old-fashioned. I don't believe in some sort of glorious city to which we're all going when we die; the place wouldn't be big enough to hold us all anyway." Many modern thinkers reject the images of The Revelation because they are not reasonable. Unfortunately, our hyper-rationalism steals from us the sense of mystery that these pictures are intended to convey. Too easily we Christians let our society's way of thinking determine ours—and such scientific quantifying (turning the symbolic cubits into feet, for example) destroys the truth of the symbol. Whatever description we might offer of what it means to be in the presence of God after our death will be grossly inadequate. All our feeble, finite attempts to comprehend the greatness of a relationship with God himself (unmarred by human sin and evil's corruption) can only stir up longing in us for the final fulfillment of its promise.

In my "Literature of the Bible" course at the University of Idaho, I gave an assignment to write a theme on what heaven would be like. One of my students, now a strong Christian leader and faithful man of God, represented it as a vast desert around which he would travel alone on a huge motorcycle. I'm sure that he would modify that picture now to include his beloved wife and daughter, too, but his sketch demonstrated that he understood the point. That which gave him greatest happiness on earth was just a foretaste of the pure Joy of heaven that he would someday experience.[1]

In one joke, a man couldn't accept the idea of a life after death in the presence of God. He said to a believer, "Do you mean to tell me that there is really going to be a city where the streets are paved with gold?" His believing friend answered, "I just know that when we are finally with God all the right values will be restored. Do you think gold is important now? After we die and learn the true meaning of it, we're just going to walk on the stuff."

That joke illustrates how we must understand the descriptions of The Revelation. What does it mean that the streets are paved in gold? Certainly, they signify great splendor, and they invite our imaginations to run freely as we contemplate the wonder of life in God's presence. They invite us also to realize that our conceptions are grossly inadequate and that our human values someday will be put into proper perspective. What we think most worthy of praise now is but a mere (and marred) foretaste of the true reality of God's creative glory.

All the dimensions and jewels and gold of the beautiful city prepare us for this central climax: there is no need for a temple in the new Jerusalem because the Lord God Almighty and the Lamb are its temple. The seer's use at this point of such a full name for God reminds us not only of his fulfillment of the First Testament covenant (LORD/Yahweh) and of his power over all that is (Almighty), but also of the suffering of the Lamb, whose sacrifice makes it possible for us to be in the city—that is, with God and his people—at all.

These names also reveal why a temple is not required. We will no longer need a place to worship nor a time set aside explicitly to focus on what our God is like. Rather, we will always be enjoying his very presence and can join the living creatures and the elders and the angels in falling at the foot of his throne. Similarly, not even the natural lights of the heavens will be required (much less human inventions) because all darkness will be gone—cast into the lake of fire. The radiance of God's presence will illumine the city, and the lamp of the Lamb will enable us to see clearly and to understand.

Once again we must pause to reflect on the significance of this message for our times of suffering and for our relationships with the weak and afflicted in our midst. This time my reflection is stirred by the constant memory of an exquisite choir anthem based on this text. In a delicately simple setting that ends with the words from Revelation 21:23 and 22:5, the composer Paul Manz had poured out his soul onto a coffee-shop napkin, while nearby in the hospital his infant son lay dying. In the darkness of his anguish Manz yearned intensely for the victory of the Lamb and for a clarity of hope, so he called for Jesus quickly to come and bring the light of his presence.

By the time Manz was done composing, his son had taken an unexpected turn for the better—and now, a grown man, serves as a pastor. Moreover, the father's vision of the meaning of eternal life, born out of the pain of his helplessness, remains in his music gently to invite us all to a deeper appreciation of the Lamb's light when we get too attracted to the neon ones.[2]

Revelation 22 begins with the pictures of the river of life, the tree with its 12 months of fruit and its leaves for the healing of the nations, the presence of God to remove the curse, and the constant ministering of those who are his servants. They are able at last to see his face, and they carry his name on their foreheads, as they reign forever in his light.

All these images work together to create a tremendous hope and to stir up longing in us for the abundant life, a life thoroughly nourished, well watered, and healed. All the conflicts of the past are over, and now people live together equally, serving God in his presence. Pictures such as these inspire our work in this present world. Since this is what the kingdom is going to be like when we experience it fully in God's own presence, then our lifestyle now, which is to be a reflection of the reign of Christ at this time, must seek the same ends. Our work as the people of God, in our present imperfect service, is to bring healing to the nations, to be counteracting the curse, to be reaping the nourishment of God's living water and fruitful tree of life.

Sometimes there is a tendency among Christians to focus so much on heaven that we lose sight of God's commands for life now in this world. Certainly it is right for us to look forward to the day when we will know Jesus face-to-face, but in the meanwhile there are many ways in which we can participate in his purposes to bring healing to the nations. Nourished by his present reign in our lives, we are challenged to be ambassadors of his kingdom and bearers of its reality.

What aspects of our present world urgently need our witness to principles of his kingdom? For example, God's invitation to bring healing to the nations causes us to couple our Christian witness to the salvation in Jesus Christ with careful efforts at peacemaking. Our words about God's grace are more easily perceived as true when our lives seek to manifest that grace faithfully.

The picture also intensifies my concern for the hungry of the world. God purposes to nourish people spiritually with the water of life as well as to provide for their material needs—to provide food for them rather than weapons of the curse. Because Jesus commands us to love and feed our enemies, it grieves me that our world spends so much of its wealth on weapons of destruction when so many people are dying of starvation and malnutrition-related diseases. When the kingdom of God determines our priorities, we are empowered to live the Gospel in ways that bring the reality of the kingdom to our world. Our ethics are an integral part of growing to understand the meaning of salvation and eternal life, for the reign of Christ is not some far-off future event. It begins to take place now in the reign of the servants.

We don't dare dismiss too lightly the words that close this section of The Revelation. Right after the beautiful pictures of the new city, the holy Jerusalem, the seer records this message from the angel: "These words are faithful and true," for "the Lord, the God of the spirits of the prophets, sent His angel to show to His bond-servants the things which must shortly take place" (22:6 NASB). In the first century those words called the suffering Christians to new hope and renewed action in living out the kingdom of God in spite of persecution. In our time, similarly, they urge us to live the truth of God's promises. The angel has been sent to 20th-century servants, too, so that we might know what is soon to take place and how we can participate in it. (We recall our questions from chapter 22, that the "How long?" is changed by the answer to "In the meanwhile?")

Immediately after the angel's words about truth and trustworthiness, the Christ himself speaks and promises that he is coming quickly. How blessed are the ones who heed the words of the prophecy of this book! As we wait for his coming, our time is not to be spent in useless speculation about how and when he will come or how to literalize the 1,000-year reign and the tribulation. Rather, we are to be busy keeping the words of the book—following the warnings sent to the seven churches and still applicable to situations in our times; recognizing the presence of evil in this world but praising God for his lordship anyway; faithfully enduring with biblical patience the tribulations we must suffer in order that we might participate in the suffering work of the kingdom; and serving as priests for the world.

The trouble throughout the centuries has been that Christianity has not found the proper balance between heaven and earth in its perspectives. To be too heavenly minded is to be no earthly good. If all we do is speculate about what it might be like when we finally get to the holy city, we will not be involved in the present work of the kingdom. The question must rather be how we are to *be* the holy city now.

In our day perhaps the threat is greater to err on the other side, to get so involved in trying to remedy the situation of this world (which will someday pass away anyway) that we lose track of the heavenly city for which we are headed. If our relationship with God does not motivate our present service, then it will not last, for we will have lost our first love. However, if we serve out of adoration and genuine worship of the Lord God Almighty and the Lamb that was slain, then our hatred of false doctrine and our patience and our works will be commended.

Blessed are those in the process of keeping the words of this book—those who faithfully live according to the kingdom as they wait for its grand fulfillment.

Notes

1. One of the best descriptions of the Joy of heaven in all of literature is found at the end of C. S. Lewis's children's tale *The Last Battle* (New York: Macmillan Publishing Co., Inc., 1956), pp. 158–74.
2. Paul Manz, "E'en So, Lord Jesus, Quickly come," St. Louis: Concordia Publishing House, 1954.

30

"Come!": Living Now in the Coming Victory

Please refer often to Revelation 22:8–21 as you study this chapter.

I needed a place to finish the rough draft of this book. There was a possibility that I could stay alone in my grandfather's home while my parents took him on a brief vacation, but the neighborhood wasn't very safe, and I was a bit worried because my health was not too stable. It is terribly hard for me to ask for help, but finally I turned to some dear friends from the first congregation I had ever served. Hesitantly requesting to work in their home for a few days, I was greatly relieved to hear their enthusiastic "Come!"

I especially appreciated the gift of that "come" a few nights later when winds of 90 miles an hour lashed the Wisconsin countryside, and a tornado just 25 miles away killed 8 people, injured more than 50, and destroyed an entire town. Throughout that night I thanked God that I was not alone, but that I had friends to awaken me and take me to the basement for safety.

So many other times, too, the word *come* has brought immense "come-fort" or relief from pain—like the time when I desperately needed an encouraging hug and one of my professors in graduate school opened his arms wide and gently said, "Come." We all need to belong, to be accepted, to be invited, to be desired, to be welcomed, to be loved, to be cherished—and the word *come* speaks to all those needs. In all our eccentricities (like my strange, restless habits and frequent outbursts on the piano during rough-draft writing), in all our pain (when we need a hug), in our confusions (over who to be and what to do), the word *come* invites us to peace and hope and strength.

Our last section of The Revelation focuses around the invitation "come." In response to the announcement of Jesus that he is coming quickly (22:7 and 12), that precious word is spoken by the Spirit and the bride, by the ones who hear, and by the seer who announces that all who are thirsty are welcomed (v. 17). Finally, on behalf of all the longing saints, the seer prays that their Lord Jesus would come (v. 20).

Truly, when we are burdened and persecuted, we learn the depth of the word *come.* When we are defenseless, we must ask our Defender to come; when we struggle endlessly with the simple tasks of life, we look forward eagerly to the invitation to come to rest. Sometimes if we lack the human resources to meet our basic needs,we become more aware of the thirst that yearns to be satisfied and waits to be bidden to come.

Our section begins with the seer so overwhelmed with gratitude for the gifts of these visions that he falls down at the angel's feet to worship the one who had shown them to him. His action and the angel's response renew again the previous warning in 19:10 to keep our gratitude properly directed. (This reminds us again of the necessity of theocentrism with which this book began.) Too easily we turn to the human agents who bring us comfort or take care of us and thereby do not appropriately recognize the source of all good things in God. I do not mean, of course, that we should not be grateful to his human representatives, but we must watch lest our relationships with them get idolatrous. God alone we are to worship, not the creatures he made and empowered for his service. Once again we are reminded that together all of us are equal bondservants and equally in need of constant reorientation so that we keep worship focused where worship is due.

In contrast to the instruction to Daniel (8:26), the seer is told to keep the words of the prophecy open and available to the people of God, for the time is near (22:10). Verse 11 does not mean that we human beings are fatalistically doomed to continue in our wrongdoing or filthiness or that we can gloat in our righteousness or holiness. Rather, we must continually recognize that our deeds issue from the kind of character we are developing. We cannot be satisfied with our present state of holiness, but we will want faithfully to keep practicing the principles of the kingdom of God now already during the present reign of Christ.

Such an ethics of character, let me emphasize, is not fatalistic, as if we had no choice about whether we would select right or wrong. Rather, the text reminds us that each of our choices reinforces the character that is developing in us. If grace reigns and we make virtuous choices, then we will continue to develop habits of virtue. On the other hand, our bad attitudes and actions reinforce the unfolding of evil. Thus, if we continue to do wrong, our character will become more and more vile.

We easily recognize this state of affairs in our lives when we fall out of some worthwhile habits—for example, of letter writing or exercise or whatever. When we stop staying in touch with our friends, we find it terribly difficult to get back into the habit. When we've broken our disciplines for physical fitness, it is hard to force ourselves back into the pain required to get into shape again.

That is why it is so important that we recognize the present reign of Christ—his 1,000-year reign that has been going on for almost 2,000 years. Unless we know the profound importance of each human act as appropriate for our participation in the kingdom or a violation of its ethics, we will not take seriously the task of our constant faithfulness and deliberate intentionality in this present world. Are we choosing the kingdom values whenever we shop? in the way we use our leisure time? in our selection of occupation? in our attitude toward the community of saints in which we are growing?

While in graduate school I especially appreciated the opportunity to participate in a vibrant congregation. The people in the parish demonstrated profoundly the meaning of Christian community in the way they prayed for each other, pursued the lifestyle of Jesus, and cared for those in need. Steeped in a rich tradition of faithful attention to the Scriptures, their deliberate commitment to following Jesus as peacemakers and justice builders nurtured the kind of Christian character that I long to exhibit.

Remember, though, that life in the kingdom is hinged to the one who is coming soon. All that is good must necessarily be seen as the work of his hand through us. Consequently, when he brings his reward, he will give to each according to what has been done. After all, he is the Alpha and Omega, the first and last, the beginning and end, the one who makes it possible for us to choose all the good that comes from him. The ones who are blessed are the ones who have washed their robes in his blood, who have been given by his grace the right to eat of the nourishing fruit of the tree of life, and who are thereby strengthened for the tasks he gives. These are the participants in the new city (22:12–14).

Once again, however, we are reminded that such things as magic arts, sexual immorality, murder, idolatry, and falsehood have no place in the kingdom. This is the constant testimony of Jesus, who calls us to an alternative lifestyle not patterned after these sins that characterize the society around us. To be involved in such things puts us outside the kingdom of Christ.

The combination of this list of sinners who have no place in the city (v. 15) and the proclamation by Jesus that he has sent his angel to testify these things for the churches (v. 16) urges us again to recognize the importance of the Christian community. The positive purpose of church discipline is to remind members of the body that certain actions lie outside the realm of the kingdom—not to push people out for sinful behavior, but to declare that these are actions that do not characterize the people of God. The church invites everyone to choose whether or not they want to participate in the moral life of God's community. Those who do not, those who persist in idolatry, sexual immorality, magic arts, murder, and falsehood, have chosen to belong to a different sort of society from the community of the bride who says, "Come."

These verses, which compare those who have washed their robes and therefore eat from the tree of life with those who practice the five sorts of sins that lie outside the kingdom, remind us that we are constantly involved in the spiritual battle that has dominated the entire book of The Revelation. Jesus is indeed Lord, but, as long as the forces of evil continue in opposition to him, we will have to endure constantly the struggle of our sainthood.

In 22:16 Jesus suddenly refers to himself as "the Root and the Offspring of David and the bright Morning Star." The images come from Isaiah 11:1 and Numbers 24:17, where the contexts emphasize the sevenfold spirit that was given to the offspring of the root of Jesse and the fact that Balaam could not curse the chosen people of God. These images underline the truth and wisdom of the testimony of Jesus, and they remind us that his first coming was long foretold, even by enemies of Israel. Now again the promise of his Second Coming brings hope for a brighter day and the ending of the darkness.

The two images also carry us back to earlier portions of The Revelation. In 5:5, the title "Root of David" was used when the Lion-Lamb was first introduced as the one able to break the seals and to reign. The title "Morning Star" recalls Christ's promise to the church at Thyatira that he would be with them (2:28).

We are eager, therefore, to respond to the Spirit's invitation to come. God's people have continued throughout the ages to be the bride saying, "Come." We enter into her tradition and join "all the ones who hear" in passing on the summons to others. We respond both by coming and by swelling the chorus of those saying, "Come."

The invitation (v. 17) to each one who is thirsty, to all who desire to receive the free gift of the water of life, ushers us back to Isaiah 55:1–2, where these phrases are first used. Several appropriate aspects must be noted here.

First of all, by means of an unusual combination of singular words for "each" and verbs that are plural, the prophet Isaiah literally says in Hebrew, "Let each one/all of you come." We each accept God's invitation as individuals, yet we come together as a community. We need each other for the coming, though no one can receive God's gracious gifts for another.

Furthermore, the Isaiah text develops its point by declaring that we can come and "buy without money and without price." To offer us the gift of the water of life was costly for God; it required the sacrifice of the Lamb who was slain. The gift had to be purchased, but its cost to us is free. We dare never take it for granted, therefore, as if the gift were worthless, nor dare we get all caught up in our own efforts to earn the gift or to deserve it or to pay God back for it.

This is especially important when we bear in mind the previous verses in Revelation 22 about our deeds and moral character. The paradox is that all these things are gifts to us, to be received totally with thanksgiving and in absolute weakness, but we do have the ability to choose the direction of our character development and to reject the gifts God would freely give us.

We might refuse to listen to the bride's calling—maybe we don't like the way the church has borne its tradition. We might refuse to acknowledge our thirst—perhaps we think the pleasures of the world satisfy it well enough. We might refuse to drink the only water that will quench our thirst—perhaps we are afraid of the plunge into commitment it asks of us. All these are our own choices for response. On the other hand, if we accept the gift of life-giving water, it is through no merit on our own, no great ability to choose that which is right, for this ability, too, is a free gift from God. That is why the word *come* is so precious. It simply invites us into Christ's waiting and welcoming arms.

Verses 18–19 warn us about the seriousness of The Revelation's prophecy. We are admonished not to take anything from it, lest we lose our place in the holy city, nor dare we add anything to it, lest God add to us the plagues. This rebuke takes us back to the emphasis on theocentrism with which we began our study together. We dare not presume to be God that we might add to what he has to tell us about his purposes.

This warning is especially urgent when some interpreters add to The Revelation a specificity about the end times. Jesus commanded us not to chase after such things. To add such interpretations when we have no biblical basis causes us to deserve the plagues poured out on those who raised rebellious hands against the reign of God.

Moreover, we are not to take away from the words of life, because then we will not be able to be nourished by them. This caution is singularly appropriate when many contemporary theologians want to give up the vision of the heavenly city. Certainly we must recognize the symbolism of the vision, that none of us can really know what form, ultimately, our relationship with God will take. However, we dare not mislay the hope of the final defeat of the Satanic opposition and the eventual triumph of the purposes of God. Those concepts nourish us and create in us the ability to continue patiently and faithfully in the struggles of our times of suffering.

Certainly God isn't up in heaven saying, "Now you better behave or I'm going to get you." Rather, he wants us to realize that to read The Revelation with *anthropo*centric eyes causes us to miss some of its blessings and to add to ourselves plagues of worries and fears that we do not need to carry. We are most blessed when we simply accept all that we can learn from The Revelation of God's purposes and not try to subtract anything that we don't understand nor to add what we want to make more specific. In short, we are blessed when we bow before the mysteries of God.

Appropriately, then, The Revelation ends with a statement of longing. For the third time Jesus promises that he is coming soon, and the hearts of his people cry out, "Yes, it is true! Amen! Come, Lord Jesus!" In the context of the first-century church, those phrases no doubt were a request for him soon to exert his lordship over the entire world and to rescue his people from the sufferings they were presently undergoing. That is why they are followed by the assurance that in the meantime grace is sufficient to sustain us in the struggles. Truly it is so: the sufficiency of the grace of Jesus as he exerts his lordship in this time will enable us to wait until he comes.

Only when we are weak and do not rely on our own strength are we able to keep this paradox in the best balance. Consumed with longing for the coming of Jesus, we yet know that in the meanwhile grace will be sufficient to sustain us.

I have written many of these comments about the lessons to be learned in our weakness because in my own struggles I have not learned them very well. Mentors like Tim and Linden and others who have entered my life over the years continue to teach me the need for weakness and the sufficiency of grace as we wait for Jesus to come. All of us in the Christian community need to learn in our various sufferings how to say "come" and how to respond by coming.

While we are waiting, these are the invitations: Come. Trust. Be graced. Long for the coming of Jesus and his ultimate triumph over evil. In the meanwhile, know his lordship in your weakness.

31

Qualities for a Theology of Weakness: Perspectives from The Revelation on Suffering

We live in a world that makes a god of strength and power, of being most important and best. Tragically, so many churches have become so caught up in our society's success and victory philosophy that U.S. Christians rarely speak a prophetic word to the world. We do not stand as an alternative community, offering a model of a different lifestyle under Christ's lordship. Individually and collectively, we have chosen too often to go after the chariots of Egypt rather than rely on the victory of God (see, for example, Is. 30:15–18 and Matt. 5:3–16). We have forgotten that God's Word still applies today, to be lived and proclaimed. We are called, as were the earliest Christians, to live by depending only on God, resisting the idolatries of the world around us, and yet compassionately offering the citizens of that world a message of hope.

The book of Revelation, written to God's people suffering in a time of persecution, has offered us clear guidance for such a life of dependence. The following paragraphs summarize the lessons that we have learned from The Revelation about the theology of weakness critically needed to resist our world's idolatries.

1. We have gained from The Revelation a deep sense of the sovereignty of God, the lordship of the Christ. He has been proclaimed as the King of kings and Lord of lords. We have seen his power and ability to defeat Satan and all the forces of evil. Though Satan is released to vent his final fling, his last assault on the people of God is easily crushed, and he and all his hosts are sent forever into

the lake of fire. The Revelation offered to the believers of the first century the profound assurance that, in spite of all appearances to the contrary, God was still in control of world history. We desperately need to recover that assurance and confident hope in our time. The secret to its recovery lies in turning our perspectives away from the anthropocentrism with which we are infected and in becoming again, like the saints of old, a people characterized by theocentricity.

2. We have gained a deeper awareness of the intensity of the battle. C. S. Lewis' old dictum that we can make two mistakes about Satan—either to take him too seriously or not to take him seriously enough—is most certainly true. Our first lesson about the effective sovereignty of God enables us not to take the powers of evil too seriously, for we know that in the end God will triumph. This second lesson enables us to take them seriously enough. We must acknowledge that we are in a strenuous and continuous battle against the hosts of evil. Satan might have been bound at the cross so that he cannot fully control things, but he and his cohorts are busily at work, wreaking havoc in this world, corrupting that which is good, deceiving the people of the earth and leading them astray into all kinds of false values and idolatries and self-centeredness. We must be vigilant against all forms of evil and be conscious in our daily decisions so that we choose between the purposes of the kingdom of God and the misleadings of the satanic hosts. Every action will be one or the other.

3. A third lesson stems from the combination of the first two. Because Jesus is Lord in spite of the powers of evil, we yearn for a greater willingness to endure suffering patiently. We have learned a new meaning for patience in situations that cannot be changed. Because biblical patience invites us to look for the presence of the Lord even in our contrary circumstances, we do not ask merely how long it will be till things are different, but we seek to learn who he is and how he enables us to respond in the midst of our suffering.

4. We have learned, therefore, the value of our sufferings and of being weak—of accepting that weakness in order that we might more thoroughly learn to depend on the sufficiency of God's grace. We have recognized that we Christians do not faithfully perform our task by seeking to be powerful and to overcome by force the oppo-

sition of the world around us. Rather, we are called to a new gentleness, a submissive humility, a gracious integrity that enables us to stand true to the principles of the kingdom of God—not in an obnoxious way opposing the world's values, but in the compassionate offering of a better alternative, a lifestyle that awaits its eventual vindication.

5. Of necessity, these first four lessons have led us to recognize the importance of the Christian community and all its members. We have seen our need to learn these lessons of weakness from whoever might know them best. We have appreciated the importance of encouraging everyone—including the handicapped, the infirm, the elderly, and the poor—to offer to our communities their gifts of insight and spiritual patience, their ability to transform the struggles of life into periods of hope, and their understanding of the lordship of Christ in the midst of afflictions. We have also seen the vast failure of our communities to make use of everyone's gifts, to nourish the equality of all of God's servants among us, to concentrate seriously on the wholeness of the body of Christ and the integral relationships of all its parts.

We have learned from the suffering church of the first century our great need for each other. The letters to the seven churches, which deal with seven different kinds of problems that we all evidence in greater and lesser degrees, remind us that we always need each other to find a better balance of love and clear doctrine and moral purity. Especially we need the gifts of those who depend on God in their limitations so that we might learn to be a church of weakness, effectively participating in the sufferings of Jesus in a culture of power.

6. As we learn to live such a theology of weakness, we must walk a careful line between the dangers of cynicism and despair. Concentrating too much on the opposition of Satan and the forces of evil will foster great cynicism. We will never expect any good to come out of anything. Concentrating only on the difficulty of patience in the face of all this opposition will lead to despair. How can we keep on going if we will never be able to accomplish God's purposes, to bring his kingdom to bear on this world?

The solution to keeping the necessary balance is to remain carefully theocentric, to concentrate on the hope that is ours because

Jesus is Lord. Such a hope can never be disappointed. It does not look for immediate victory, but it does acknowledge the perfect power and wisdom of his sovereignty. In his time and according to his best purposes, all evil will ultimately be defeated. For that end we continue to yearn—and to work, since we have been given the task of witnessing to his sovereignty in the meanwhile.

7. Finally, we have seen that such a theology of weakness creates a life of great Joy. Even in the midst of the direst sufferings, we can know the Joy of our relationship with the sovereign Christ and of his infinite love for us. We have sung with the elders and the living creatures many new songs of praise. We have exulted in the Lamb's worthiness to receive all honor and glory and power and thanksgiving and strength and wisdom and might into the aeons of the aeons. Amen! It shall be so—and in the assurance of that amen we rejoice with an exceedingly great Joy, which our human existence cannot otherwise know.

Such Joy characterizes the Christian community that knows its place and eagerly awaits the consummation of its visions. Such is the Joy of those who recognize that the dwelling of God will someday be with us thoroughly, but that now, in the meanwhile, he tabernacles among us in our weakness. Such is the Joy of those who love their king and submit willingly to his sovereign presence—his 1,000-year reign—in their lives and struggles.

These are the characteristics of a theology of weakness. Our world mocks such a theology, but that does not in the slightest detract from its truth.

BIBLIOGRAPHY

Boring, Eugene M. *Revelation*. Louisville: John Knox Press, 1989.

Botts, Timothy R. *Doorposts*. Wheaton, IL: Tyndale House Publishers, Inc., 1986.

Chilton, Bruce and J. I. H. McDonald. *Jesus and the Ethics of the Kingdom*. Grand Rapids, MI: Wm. B. Eerdmans Publishing Co., 1987.

Dawn, Marva J. "The Concept of 'The Principalities and Powers' in the Works of Jacques Ellul." University of Notre Dame: Ph.D. dissertation, 1992.

_____. *The Hilarity of Community: Romans 12 and the Meaning of the Church*. Grand Rapids, MI: Wm. B. Eerdmans Publishing Co., 1992.

_____. *I'm Lonely, LORD—How Long?: The Psalms for Today*. San Francisco: Harper and Row, 1983.

_____. *Keeping the Sabbath Wholly: Ceasing, Resting, Embracing, Feasting*. Grand Rapids, MI: Wm. B. Eerdmans Publishing Co., 1989.

_____. *Sexual Character: Beyond Technique to Intimacy*. Grand Rapids, MI: Wm. B. Eerdmans Publishing Co., 1993.

Ellul, Jacques. *Apocalypse: The Book of Revelation*. George W. Schreiner, trans. New York: The Seabury Press, 1977.

_____. *The Humiliation of the Word*. Joyce Main Hanks, trans. Grand Rapids, MI: Wm. B. Eerdmans Publishing Company, 1985.

_____. *The Meaning of the City*. Dennis Pardee, trans. Grand Rapids, MI: Wm. B. Eerdmans Publishing Company, 1970.

_____. *Money and Power*. LaVonne Neff, trans. Downers Grove, IL: InterVarsity Press, 1984.

Hauerwas, Stanley. *Suffering Presence: Theological Reflections on Medicine, the Mentally Handicapped, and the Church*. Notre Dame, IN: Notre Dame Press, 1986.

Kreeft, Peter. *Making Sense Out of Suffering*. Ann Arbor, MI: Servant Books, 1986.

Lenski, R. C. H. *The Interpretation of St. John's Revelation*. Minneapolis, MN: Augsburg Publishing House, 1963.

Lewis, C. S. *The Last Battle*. New York: Macmillan Publishing Co., Inc., 1956.

Manz, Paul. "E'en So, Lord Jesus, Quickly Come." St. Louis: Concordia Publishing House, 1954.

Messiaen, Olivier. *Quatuor pour la fin du temps*. Helen Baker, trans. Musical Heritage Society recording.

Mounce, Robert H. *The Book of Revelation*. F. F. Bruce, gen. ed. *The New International Commentary on the New Testament*. Grand Rapids, MI: Wm. B. Eerdmans Publishing Co., 1977.

Mulholland, M. Robert, Jr. *Invitation to a Journey: A Road Map for Spiritual Formation*. Downers Grove, IL: InterVarsity Press, 1993.

O'Connor, Elizabeth. "Learning from an Illness," *Cry Pain, Cry Hope: Thresholds to Purpose*. Waco, TX: Word Books, 1987, pp. 114–29.

Solzhenitsyn, Alexander. *Stories and Prose Poems*. Michael Glenny, trans. New York: Farrar, Straus and Giroux, 1971.

Ugolnik, Anthony. *The Illuminating Icon*. Grand Rapids, MI: Wm. B. Eerdmans Publishing Co., 1989.